RESCUE UNDER FIRE

RESCUE UNDER FIRE

The Story of DUST OFF in Vietnam

John L. Cook

Schiffer Military/Aviation History
Atglen, PA

Book Design by Ian Robertson.

Copyright © 1998 by John L. Cook
Library of Congress Catalog Number: 97-80322

Printed in the United States of America.
ISBN: 0-7643-0461-5

We are interested in hearing from authors with book ideas on related topics.

Published by Schiffer Publishing Ltd.
77 Lower Valley Road
Atglen, PA 19310
Phone: (610) 593-1777
FAX: (610) 593-2002
E-mail: Schifferbk@aol.com
Please write for a free catalog.
This book may be purchased from the publisher.
Please include $3.95 postage.
Try your bookstore first.

Contents

Preface

Of all the books written about the Vietnam war, both good and bad, not a single one has focused on the role played by the men who flew the medical evacuation mis sions for the US Army. I don't know why this is the case, but it is. It seems that every aspect of this war has been studied, analyzed, dissected and probed by an endless succession of highly respected scholars, journalists and soldiers. It is absolutely incredible that no serious account has been given of that very special breed of men who flew their helicopters through enemy fire and monsoons to rescue the wounded. Countless volumes have been penned attempting to explain our strategy, or lack of it, and any number of personal accounts have been written concerning the war on the ground and the war in the air. Still, nothing has been written about the helicopter crews that saved our wounded. I have a

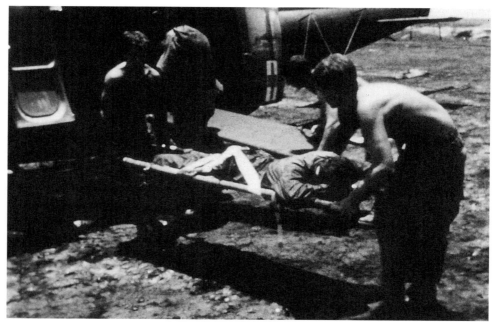

theory they may explain this neglect, but I can't prove it. Most writers and reporters that shaped the average American's view of the war while it was going on tended to focus on the negative aspects of this conflict. They did this for a variety of reasons. First, it was considered politically fashionable at the time to portray the war in bleak, stark terms and to portray American forces in a less than favorable light. Another reason most writers followed this course of action was so obvious that most Americans failed to pick up on it—it was incredibly easy. With so much death and suffering all around them, writers in the combat zone simply wrote about what they saw. It required no deeper analysis, even if the reporters were capable of providing it. We did, indeed, pay a very high price in human terms. Extremely high. Over 57,000 Americans died there. So, there was no shortage of negative material to explore and expand. However, in order to put great events in context, it is often necessary to go beyond the obvious and look very carefully at what was happening throughout the combat zone. Had this happened, those who flew the evacuation missions would have received the credit they so richly deserved. But it didn't happen because it required setting aside political and philosophical agendas and focus on what actually happened, not what we may have wanted to happen.

DUST OFF is an effort to correct this injustice and pay tribute to a magnificent group of brave, selfless men. Those seeking a grand strategy assessment or a mind-numbing discussion concerning policy issues involving the Vietnam war need to look elsewhere. This story is far too important to be diluted by such petty issues that are so dependent on time and place and personal whim.

This is not a story about anguish, self-doubt, or defeat. You will find no gloomy self analysis here. What you will find is an exceptional success story, a story created by the dedication and effort and courage of a group of ordinary Americans who performed extraordinary feats, day in and day out, saving lives. DUST OFF is a story that could have been written about any American war because it illustrates and high-lights the very best our national character has to offer—Americans risking their lives to save others. The setting is Vietnam, however, the people and events I will soon introduce you to transcends the combat zone. It has been a long time coming, but finally here is the story that should have been told a long time ago.

A Very Personal Experience With DUST OFF

I became a true believer in DUST OFF on the 15th of November, 1968. At the time, I did not know the origin of the extremely efficient evacuation system that was supporting the troops on the ground in South Vietnam. I didn't know the origin of the call sign DUST OFF, either. All I knew was what every other guy over there knew— that if we got in a world of hurt and at least one man was still able to key the mike and yell "We need a DUST OFF right now!", those Hueys with the big red crosses would come. It was about the only thing we could count on. It was better than money in the bank. The idea of DUST OFF not coming was unthinkable. The absolute certainty of DUST OFF coming was something we believed in completely. It made combat operations a hell of a lot more bearable. I realize now that this attitude was driven more by faith than fact, but it didn't change the attitude of the guys on the ground. In many ways, the belief in DUST OFF was stronger than a closely held religious conviction. We weren't absolutely certain God would listen to our prayers, or whether God had taken a position on the war, but we knew DUST OFF was with us.

On this bright, sunny day, Captain Wentworth and I were doing our job as advisors in Di-An District. He was the Deputy District Senior Advisor and I was a brand new First Lieutenant, responsible for running the Phoenix Program in Di An.

We were with a company of South Vietnamese soldiers south of Binh Tri looking for Viet Cong. We were to sweep south for about three kilometers and link up with another South Vietnamese company which was in a blocking position. The idea was to flush the Viet Cong out of the thick, heavy brush and force them ahead of us, driving them into the blocking force. For this particular operation, we had asked the 1st Infantry Division for a dog team and they had provided a large German Shepherd and his handler, Sergeant Pine.

About 1 kilometer south of Binh Tri outpost, we ran into heavy resistance from the foliage—thick bushes with razor-sharp thorns grew up about three feet, then curled around themselves, creating a natural barbed-wire like barrier. These bushes slowed the operation as we carefully picked our way through them. The sun was climbing higher and the sweat started to flow. Its going to be a long day, I thought, hoping to get through the damn bushes without ruining a perfectly good set of jungle fatigues.

"No goddamn VC in his right mind would live in a place like this," Wentworth muttered as he took a long drink from his canteen. He purposely let a few drops run down his chin and then spread the cool water over his neck with his free hand. Sergeant Pine was in front of me and to the left with the scout dog. The dog seemed to be unconcerned about the whole operation, stopping only occasionally to sniff at a bush or a tree.

"That son of a bitch ain't looking for VC. He's just trying to find out if another dogs been through here pissing on trees," Wentworth complained behind me. I was beginning to agree.

Suddenly, the dog stopped and the dark brown hair on his back stood straight up. Pine unleashed the dog. The big German Shepherd took a few cautious steps forward and put his nose to the ground. This is good, I thought; the dog is about to do what he's supposed it do—find booby traps or the entrances to Viet Cong tunnels. According to Pine, this dog was one of the best in the business. That's why we had him with us on this operation. In short, the dog was a highly trained professional. We were now going to find out just how good he was. I was about to tell Wentworth we may have found a tunnel when it happened. I watched in stunned, detached amazement as the ground under the dog exploded. It appeared to happen in slow motion, the big, black cloud of smoke expanding and rolling toward me. And, for an instant, the dog became a part of the blackness, moving effortlessly upward with the cloud until he disintegrated into a black and red mist. At that point, the cloud swept over me and I became a part of it. The blast threw me 30 feet into a clump of thorn bushes.

For awhile, time ceased to exist. I don't know how long I was unconscious; it could have been only a few seconds or several minutes. When I came to, still dazed from the blast, the first thing I saw was Nghia, the Vietnamese radio operator, lying against me. I was vaguely aware of the thorns embedded in my right hand and the insistent ringing in my ears. Blood was leaking through my fatigue shirt in at least five places but I felt no real pain, only a strange sense of unreality, as if I was observing this scene from some other place.

Instinctively, I reached out to check Nghia. He was dead. Of this, I had no doubt. His eyes were open and they were staring vacantly into the bright morning sky. The radio had been blown off his back by the force of the blast, and Nghia was covered with greasy-looking blood. Wentworth was sitting a few yards away, rocking back and forth in obvious pain, watching the blood run from a large hole in his thigh. Pine was lying face down with a hole in his left calf. Wounded Vietnamese soldiers were lying all around us, casualties of a Viet Cong booby trap fashioned from a 105 mm artillery round.

Amazingly, the radio still worked, and I was able to raise the District Headquarters.

"We need a DUST OFF right now!" I shouted, putting my blind faith in the evacuation system to the test.

" Roger that," Specialist Bradford, at District Headquarters, replied. I need your location. He was a cool headed, dependable guy who would pass the request up the line immediately, but I could tell from his voice that this time he was excited. He was part of the seven man district team that both Wentworth and I belonged to. And we were close, all of us. The night before, Bradford had won five bucks from me in a poker game, and I vowed to get it back. He was a damn good poker player, much better than me. I fumbled in my side pocket for the map and pulled it out.

"Make that X-ray Tango 963 875," I replied after studying the map and making my best guess. "That's close enough. We have approximately ten wounded." That was another guess, too, and I hoped to God we didn't have any more than that. "Tell them to hurry," I added.

"Will do," Bradford replied reassuringly. "DUST OFF will be on the way." Then, violating all radio procedure, Bradford added, "Hang in there, sir. Well get you out."

While my request was being relayed to DUST OFF Control at Long Binh, we got the wounded to a tiny clearing about 100 yards away. By this time, I knew we had twelve wounded—five critical. It took ten minutes of steady carrying, pulling and dragging the bloody but still breathing men to the clearing that was going to serve as a landing zone. By now, Wentworth's leg wound had taken him out of action. I put my belt around it to stop the bleeding and told him DUST OFF would pick us up soon.

With the wounded at the landing zone, I organized a hasty perimeter with the South Vietnamese soldiers who were not wounded, fully expecting the Viet Cong to attack. As we waited under the hot sun, I wondered if DUST OFF would be able to find us. And if they found us, would they be able to land? Up to this point, I had tried to ignore my own wounds because I didn't want to think about it. But as we waited, I unbuttoned my shirt and took a look at my chest. Blood was oozing out of a lot of holes. I couldn't tell how many and I didn't want to know right then. I buttoned up my shirt and pretended that it wasn't that bad. The wounded Vietnamese were looking at me with a degree of apprehension and fear. I tried to appear as confident as I could under the circumstances. No reason to upset them any more than they already are, I thought. As I looked at this large group of wounded men, including Wentworth, I realized that we would need two helicopters. There was no was we were all going to fit on a single Huey.

Suddenly, the radio that had now become my most valuable possession, came alive. It was DUST OFF and they wanted me to mark our location with smoke. I threw a red smoke grenade into the center of the clearing and waited. This effort sent a sharp pain through my left arm. That's when I knew I had at least one hole in my arm, too.

"I identify red," came the calm response from the pilot.

"That's us," I answered, breathing a sigh of relief.

Then I heard the distinctive whoop-whoop-whoop of the Huey. There is no other sound like that in the world. You always hear a Huey before you see it. At the bottom of the small clearing, surrounded by trees, our field of view was limited. We couldn't see the helicopter as it approached but we could hear it coming and that was a reassuring sound. An instant later, the Huey was directly above us. I looked up and saw the big red cross on the bottom of the helicopter. Without question, that was one of the most beautiful sights I had ever seen.

Within seconds, the aircraft descended into the landing zone and we began loading the most seriously wounded first. In less than two minutes, I had nine of the seriously wounded on board and it looked to me like the helicopter was full. I walked over to the right side of the helicopter and opened the co-pilot's door. He was a very young Warrant Officer, no more than nineteen years old.

"I think you've got a load!" I shouted over the noise of the main rotor. "The rest of us will wait for the next DUST OFF!"

"No disrespect, Lieutenant," he replied, shouting directly into my ear, "but I suggest you get your ass on board along with the rest of the wounded. This is it!"

"Look," I tried to explain. "I've got three other Vietnamese out here and myself. Can you take us all?"

"Well, we'll damn sure find out pretty soon, wont we?" he told me, smiling confidently. "So, lets get it done. I don't like sitting here giving Charlie a target."

This is one crazy son of a bitch, I thought, but he just might be right. With that, I helped load the rest of the wounded and climbed in, squeezing in between the men lying on the floor. It was tight, but we all fit. When we were all aboard, the Huey slowly lifted out of the clearing. With the landing skids barely clearing the tree tops, we were on our way to the 93d Evacuation Hospital at Long Binh. The medic and crew chief went to work immediately, applying bandages and hooking up blood transfusions. Each of us was examined and our condition reported to the pilot. By the time we arrived at Long Binh, the 93d was ready for us. The total elapsed time from wounding to evacuation had been only 45 minutes.

The medic on board the DUST OFF directed the unloading. The most seriously wounded were taken off first and rushed into the hospital. By now I was stiffening up, and the pain was getting pretty bad. However, I wanted to make it on my own as far as possible. With the aid of a medic supporting me, I hobbled across the tarmac. As I limped toward the hospital, I looked back at the DUST OFF still sitting on the landing pad. I wanted to go back and thank the crew for what they had done, but there was no time. The moment had passed, and I knew it. The engine was already revving up for the next mission. All I could do was wave, hoping the wave conveyed our appreciation. Apparently, that was enough. The co-pilot, who was, without question, crazy, gave me a thumbs up. And, I swear to God, he was still smiling.

On that November morning I had, quite by accident, contributed to the DUST OFF legacy. Everything I had been told about this remarkable organization had been true. I called them, and they had come. At the time, however, I had no way of knowing what a remarkable accomplishment this was. Being a young lieutenant, I assumed that it had always been this way. Quite naturally, I was grateful for being rescued and was impressed with the speed and efficiency in which it was carried out, but what I failed to realize was how remarkable this organization really was. I didn't know that it was a miracle that DUST OFF even existed. During the course of the war, this scene would be repeated thousands of times by the crews of the medical evacuation helicopters.

Now, all these years later, I have done the very best job I am capable of in telling their story. I have researched thousands of documents, and talked to as many former DUST OFF crew members as I could find. Now, I know enough about this remarkable organization to tell its story. However, there is a certain irony to my research. The only thing I regret is that I have not been able to identify the crew that saved my life, particularly that irreverent young Warrant Officer. Maybe that's the way it's supposed to be. I like to think that he and his crew survived the war, but I have no way of knowing that. In any event, it is with profound gratitude and deep respect that I tell their story. It is a story well worth telling.

Lieutenant Colonel John L. Cook
US Army (Retired)
Owings, Maryland
1997

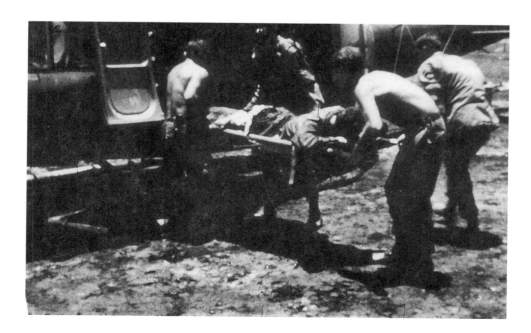

1

Welcome to Vietnam
(1962: Up Against the System)

T he ancient, four engine DC6 was only two hours out of Travis Air Force Base, California, when the trouble began. The number one engine, outboard on the left wing, started leaking oil. Captain John Temperelli Jr., US Army, watched with curiosity when the Air Force pilot, Captain Curt Ferrar, entered the cabin, smiled at the 33 Army passengers, looked out the left side of the aircraft for a few seconds, and casually returned to the cockpit. Temperelli's curiosity immediately turned to suspicion. As a helicopter pilot,

First Team: Members of the original 57th Medical Detachment that arrived in April 1962. Despite the smiles, the first months were rough—unexpected and unwanted they had to put up with makeshift quarters and endless bureaucratic muddies. From left to right: Capt. John Temperelli, Jr.; Sgt. First Class Alvin Cooper; SP5 Aungst, medic; and SP5 Sziglagyl, Crew Chief. The small monkey Aungst is holding was the unit's mascot, "Huey." Shortly after this photo was taken, the helicopter in the background crashed due to contaminated fuel.

he fully expected things to go wrong when they could. He took a look for himself. What he saw confirmed his concern—a stream of oil as thick as a lead pencil was flowing from the outboard engine, polluting the clear, blue sky over the Pacific. Fifteen minutes later, after assessing that the problem was serious, the pilot, Captain Ferrar, announced that he was returning to Travis. Temperelli breathed a sigh of relief, but he kept his eye on the number one engine, just in case.

From this most inauspicious beginning, the legacy of DUST OFF was born. However, on this April afternoon in 1962, John Temperelli was not thinking about a legacy. All he wanted to do was get his unit, the 57th Medical Detachment, from Fort George G. Meade, Maryland, to Nha Trang, Republic of South Vietnam. Temperelli desperately wanted to get his small unit, which consisted of 29 men and five brand new UH-1A Huey helicopters to Vietnam. He had been told that the American effort in South Vietnam was in desperate need of the kind of service he and his men could provide. His would be the very first helicopter ambulance unit to join the war. But it was proving to be difficult just to get out of the United States. Later, the military would develop much more efficiency in moving men to the combat zone, but that was still to come, out there somewhere in the future.

In the spring of 1962, Vietnam was not much of a war. In fact, it could be argued that it wasn't a real war at all, at least not for America. US policy makers were divided and uncertain as to just how far the nation should go in supporting the struggling democracy of South Vietnam. Everyone agreed that something needed to be done; however there was no clear, concise policy as to what that something should be. This failure of defining objectives would be the hallmark of the Vietnam war for the next thirteen years. While America vacillated over what should be done, the South Vietnamese military was involved, on a daily basis, with various enemy communist forces, including home-grown Viet Cong and even North Vietnamese regulars on occasion. And, every day, the South Vietnamese military was taking casualties. But it wasn't Americas war—at least not yet. In 1962, the United States had only 8,000 military advisors on the ground in South Vietnam, spread very thin throughout the countryside. No one could have predicted that, in less than six years, the US would have over half a million men on the ground. All of that, however, was still to come. In 1962, Vietnam was not a major concern to the average American. America was at peace, the economy was strong and the future looked very bright . The nation was in love with its young president, who kept telling them that their destiny was to spread democracy throughout the world and to put a man on the moon by the end of the decade. John F. Kennedy was in his second year as president, BONANZA was the top rated television program in the country, John Glenn had just become the first American to circle the earth in Friendship 7, and the Green Bay Packers were champions of the National Football League. In short, the good times were rolling again and America wanted to roll with them. Most Americans could not even find Vietnam on a map, even if they were interested, because most maps at the time simply listed Vietnam as part of Indo-China. All of this would change of course, but it would take time.

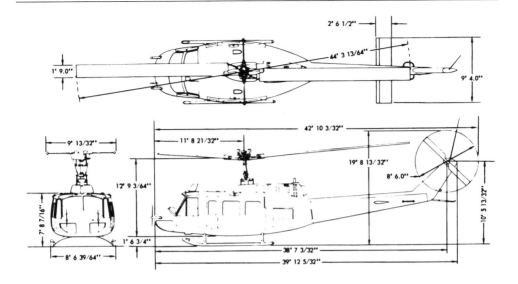

U. S. Army UH-1D

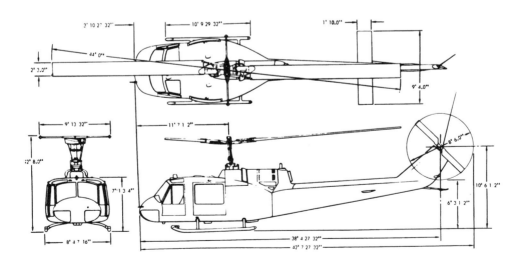

U. S. Army UH-1B

Against this backdrop, the old DC6 lumbered back to Travis for some much needed repair work. The next day, they departed once again and arrived at Hickam Field, Hawaii, without incident. However, there was another delay at Hickam. The crew had to rest and there was more maintenance work required. From Hickam, the DC6 flew a course to Wake Island for refueling and then on to Clark Air Force Base in the Philippines. There were more delays at Clark. By now, the members of the 57th had grown accustomed to delays and decided to put the time they had to good purpose. While the DC6 was being nursed back into service, the pilots of the 57th went on a scrounging mission. They were looking for maps of Vietnam and they were in luck. In one of the hangers, they found a set of World Aeronautic Charts (WAC) and some Jepson maps for Southeast Asia. These finds would prove extremely valuable when they arrived at Nha Trang. At Nha Trang in April, 1962, map coverage consisted of 1:500,000 scale maps, 1926 vintage, which put all of Vietnam—both north and south—on a 3 by 5 foot wall chart! These one over the world scale maps made it almost impossible for a helicopter, flying just above the tree tops at 80 knots to make a successful pick-up in unfamiliar, mountainous terrain, but this was precisely what was going to be expected of Temperelli's unit.

Capt. John Temperelli, Jr., the first commander of the 57th Medical Detachment flying a UH-1A during an early evacuation mission near Nha Trang in July 1962. Temperelli had brought the 57th's innovative air ambulance service to Vietnam from Fort Meade, MD, in April 1962. His early struggles to get the top brass to accept the validity of the DUST OFF concept made its later success possible.

Such massive breakdowns in critical logistics were common in 1962. American units assigned to Vietnam during this period were pretty much on their own. There was no effective policy that outlined what the units being sent to Vietnam needed to bring and what would be made available to them when they arrived. Most units, such as the 57th, simply assumed the worst and tried to bring everything they owned. To their credit, Temperelli and his officers knew there would be problems to work out once they were on the ground in Nha Trang. They had no way of knowing, however, just how bad the problems would be.

Barely two months earlier at Fort Meade, Temperelli had been alerted to get ready to deploy to South Vietnam. This created a frenzied logistical effort that generated more questions than answers. Most of the questions concerned support. Where, exactly, were they going and what kind of support would they receive? No one knew, exactly. About the only specific information Temperelli received was that his unit would be attached to the 8th Field Hospital in Nha Trang. Beyond this, specifics were scarce. However, in the absence of specific guidance, the American soldier does something better than any other fighting man in the world—he improvises. When their questions went unanswered, the men of the 57th took matters into their own hands. At times, their initiative went a bit too far. In order to feed the men, the supply officer even proceeded to have a 2 1/2 ton truck converted into a mobile kitchen. When Temperelli tactfully pointed out that the 57th had no cooks, the supply officers response was equally creative. "We'll cross train the mechanics," he told Temperelli. In the end, the commander and his supply officer reached a compromise—they brought along a six months supply of C rations. No one told them about survival equipment, so they made up survival kits that included things they thought they may need. Each kit, carried in a parachute bag and placed on board the helicopters, included a machete, canned water, extra ammunition, flares, compass, a signaling mirror, blankets, and any other item the men could think of that would be helpful in a survival situation. They did the best they could with the time they had. In a lot of ways, Temperelli and his unit were pioneers. There were no other medical evacuation units operating in Vietnam to question. Nor were there many Vietnam veterans around who could address their most basic concerns. So, in the end, Temperelli and the men of the 57th had to wing it to a large degree, knowing, intuitively, that their services were desperately needed, even if there were more questions than answers and far more nagging uncertainty than any of these brave men deserved.

Finally, on the 26th of April, eight days and 9,000 miles west of Travis Air Force Base, California, the tired and wounded DC6 flew over the coast of South Vietnam. Every man on board rushed to a window for the first glimpse of Nha Trang. As the plane descended for landing, details of the landscape came into focus. Small clusters of huts became visible around the long runway. The plane continued its rapid descent, barely clearing tin-roofed houses and scraggly palm trees, threatening to make contact with the ground short of the run way. The old DC6 flared, slightly raising its nose, and a second later, the wheels touched the runway. At least the long ordeal of the flight over the Pacific was now behind them. The 57th was, more or less, on station in Vietnam. For the first time since leaving Travis, Temperelli allowed himself to relax a bit. Tired and sore, the men filed out into the bright April sun. They were about to trade the agony of the plane for a brand new agony—the heat and humidity of Southeast Asia.

As it turned out, the heat and humidity weren't the only problems facing the men of the 57th on April 26th. There were members of the 8th Field Hospital on hand to greet the plane. However, they were not there for Temperelli's unit. A team of orthopedic surgeons had made the trip from Ft. Meade with the 57th. The surgeons were expected; Temperelli and his crew were not. When Temperelli asked the young lieutenant where he and his men were to report, he was met with a blank stare.

"You knew we were coming, didn't you?" Temperelli asked.

"No sir," the lieutenant replied. "We don't know a damn thing about you."

Welcome to Vietnam, 1962. Temperelli was standing in the sun on the tarmac at Nha Trang with his seven officers and twenty-two enlisted men, his helicopters were on a ship somewhere in the Pacific, and no one within six time zones even knew he was on the ground in Vietnam.

Aside from the personal frustration and anger this response created in Captain John Temperelli, Commander of the 57th Medical Detachment (Helicopter Ambulance), it does accurately illustrate a critically important point concerning Americas early involvement in Vietnam. There was no clear, direct, understandable mission statement guiding the United States military forces in the Vietnam conflict. What was happening in Vietnam—and Washington, DC—at this time could be accurately described at mission creep—except there was no clear cut mission emanating from Washington. Defense policy was now in the hands of Robert McNamara and the whiz kids. To a large degree, this group believed that having good intentions was almost as good as having firm, solid defense policy. They were already experimenting with the concept of limited war and containment, two pieces of fuzzy thinking that would be thoroughly repudiated by the end of the war.

Thus, Temperelli's frustration and confusion was not unique to units being assigned to Vietnam during this time frame. In truth, it was all too common. During this period, Americas role in Southeast Asia was in a constant state of turmoil. Very few of the Americans there knew, with any certainty, who they worked for. Just two short months before Temperelli arrived, on the 8th of February, the United States Military Assistance Command, Vietnam (MACV), was established. Prior to MACV, the Military Assistance Advisory Group (MAAG), acted as the senior military headquarters for all units in South Vietnam. MAAG contained Army, Navy and Air Force sections, each responsible for advising and assisting its counterpart in the Vietnamese armed forces while, at the same time, assisting the chief of the advisory effort, General Timmes, in administering the Military Assistance Program. What about

June 1962, Nha Trang. Despite the living conditions, the pilots of the 57th are capable of smiling for the camera. From left to right: Captain Bob McWilliams, Captain Don Naylor, Captain Bill Hawkins (kneeling), Lieutenant Tom Jackson, Captain John Temperelli, Jr. (Commander), and Sergeant First Class Alvin Cooper.

logistical support? In theory, logistical support was supposed to be provided by the Commanding General, US Army Ryukyu Islands (USARIS), all the way back on Okinawa.

These multiple lines and layers of responsibility clearly would not work during serious combat. Rather, they represented the military's response to a lack of clear guidance from Washington—when in doubt, reorganize and build the biggest bureaucracy possible. And that is precisely what happened. The creation of MACV, under the command of General Paul Harkins, did not eliminate MAAG. MAAG was allowed to survive for advisory and operational matters supporting MACV, while responding to the Commander-in-Chief, Pacific, for the administration of the Military Assistance Program. Nothing of operational value was accomplished by retaining MAAG. MAAGs existence simply complicated an already fuzzy command structure. For example, since General Timmes (MAAG) had operational control of Army aviation units, the Army Senior Advisor assigned to a Vietnamese Corps could initiate a request for aviation support. In fact, the Vietnamese Corps Commander could initiate and plan a helicopter operation. The US advisor assigned to that Vietnamese Corps would formally transmit a request to the commanding officer of a US Army helicopter company for execution. Actual planning for such an operation thus involved the Vietnamese Corps Commander, the MAAG representative, and the commander of the helicopter company. Naturally, such a convoluted arrangement caused problems. When problems arose that could not be resolved locally between the advisor and the helicopter company commander, they were referred to General Harkins. As a result, Army aviation commanders had to deal with and satisfy, on a daily basis, the Vietnamese Army, MAAG, MACV, and the US Army Support Group. The Support Group, in turn, had to respond to the US Army, Pacific; USARYIS; and MACV.

Against this back drop, Temperelli entered the combat zone. The problems he faced were obvious and he wasn't even aware of all of them. If combat aviation units faced a hopelessly bureaucratic chain of command, how was a small medical detachment expected to function? There were no simple answers.

The disarray and confusion was not limited to the operational side of the US effort. Medical support during this period was also in chaos. The 8th Field Hospital, the unit Temperelli thought was waiting to greet him with open arms, had just opened for business in Nha Trang earlier in April, assuming responsibility for the hospitalization of all US military, dependents, and US civilians living in South Vietnam, with a secondary mission to supply all medical units in the country.

Why was the sleepy little coastal town of Nha Trang, located some 200 miles northeast of Saigon, and one of the most sparsely populated areas of the country, selected for such a critical task? Was it because the Army leadership anticipated an influx of causalities from the surrounding areas? Had some detailed analysis been performed and all indications pointed to Nha Trang as being the most strategic location for a 100 bed hospital? To understand the answers to these questions, it is important to understand and appreciate the priorities of the Army leadership in country during 1962. Quite simply, the 8th Field Hospital was ordered to Nha Trang because there was no room for it in Saigon. Where it should be located wasn't even a consideration in 1962. Space was available at Nha Trang and, to the MAAG commander, this became the deciding issue. Placing the 8th Field at Nha Trang would prove to be an extremely costly mistake, but that was still in the future.

John Temperelli had no way of knowing all this as he stood on the tarmac at Nha Trang. Had he known how ill-conceived the planning in Saigon was, he might well have put the 57th back on board the old DC6 and said, the hell with it. Call me when you get your act together. To his credit, he didn't. Instead, he insisted on seeing the commander of the 8th Field Hospital. Temperelli explained, in no uncertain terms, that he and his men were there to do a job and he expected quarters to be made available to him. Temperelli's directness paid off, more or less. Living accommodations were made available for the 57th that very afternoon—tents set up on concrete slabs. It wasn't much but, for the time being, it was home.

After three days of sitting around Nha Trang trying, unsuccessfully, to get some straight answers out of the staff of the 8th Field Hospital, Temperelli took matters into his own hands. He hopped a ride on an Air Force transport to Saigon. His objective was fairly simple. Temperelli wanted to find out exactly what he was expected to do. He started his quest in the office of the Medical Staff Advisor, Major Frank Filtch. What Filtch had planned for the 57th left Temperelli temporarily speechless. The Medical Staff Advisor had drawn up a deployment plan that placed Temperelli's five helicopters in four separate locations, strung out from the delta south of Saigon all the way up to Qui Nhon, over 90 miles north of Nha Trang.

"What do you think?" Filtch asked Temperelli.

"With all due respect, sir, it's bullshit," Temperelli replied angrily, suddenly realizing that the major didn't have a clue as to how his unit should be deployed. "We have to be close enough to each other to provide mutual support, spare parts and all that. I've got the only Hueys in country. From a purely maintenance perspective, this will not work. You've got me strung out all over the coast!"

"Well, this plan has been approved by the Support Command Commander," Filtch said, thinking this would put an end to the discussion. It didn't. Temperelli insisted on seeing the commander. After a brief delay, he was shown into the rather plush, comfortable office of Colonel Marvin Merchant, Support Group Commander.

"Major Filtch says you don't like our deployment plan for your unit, Temperelli.
What's wrong with it?" Merchant demanded.

Patiently, Temperelli explained to the colonel that the 57th was not designed to be separated helicopter by helicopter. He could not give each location a full compliment of mechanics and there was only one complete tool set for the UH-1As. Spare parts would be a real problem if Temperelli had to maintain four locations. Then there was the problem of fuel. The Huey was powered by a turbine engine which required JP-4 fuel. In 1962, there were only two locations in Vietnam that had JP4—Saigon and Nha Trang. And so it went, for over an hour as Temperelli explained why unit integrity was so important. Finally, the colonel asked Temperelli where he wanted to be located.

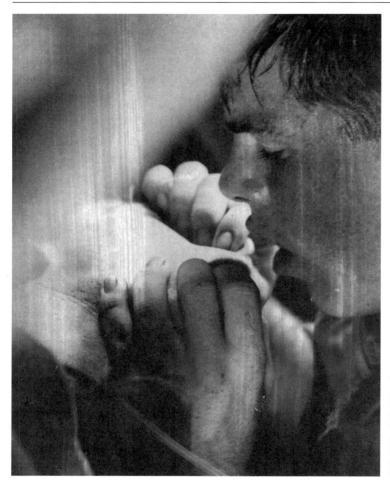

The medics that flew on medical evacuation helicopters had on primary mission: keep the wounded alive until they reached hospital. Here, mouth-to-mouth resuscitation is being administered.

"Where ever your causalities are the greatest, sir," Temperelli answered simply. The colonel turned to Major Filtch and asked where that was. Incredibly, the medical advisor did not know. This response stunned Temperelli; Colonel Merchant seemed to take it in stride. However, the admission that Saigon did not know where, precisely, most of the causalities were coming from strengthened Temperelli's case for keeping the 57th together. The meeting ended with a compromise: Temperelli would divide his helicopters between only two locations—Nha Trang and Qui Nhon. Finally, some decisions regarding the fate of the 57th were being made. Perhaps not the best decisions, but they were decisions nonetheless.

John Temperelli was learning some valuable lessons about Vietnam. First of all, even a young captain willing to stand up for what he believed in could make a difference. By fighting to keep the 57th as intact as possible, Temperelli ensured that his unit would at least receive a chance to survive and make a contribution. Another lesson he was learning the hard way involved politics, Vietnam style. At the time, political considerations far outweighed the necessity of putting together a cohesive support network capable of countering the growing communist threat. Few realized, at any level, what was about to happen in Vietnam. Fewer still had any idea concerning the best course of action. This is best illustrated by one of the key assumptions that led to the creation of MACV.

With an initial authorized strength of 216 men, MACV was viewed as a temporary headquarters that would be withdrawn once the Vet Cong were defeated. When this happened, the senior planners theorized, the Military Assistance Advisory Group (MAAG) would be restored to its former position as the principal US headquarters in South Vietnam.

This confusion was not entirely the fault of the military leadership, however. The Kennedy administration was more concerned with maintaining a flexible policy that allowed for options in Vietnam than with making a specific, focused effort designed to bring military victory. Containment of communist expansion was heard more often than winning. The emphasis was clearly on not losing South Vietnam to the communists, yet very little in the way of specific guidance was being given to the units in the field. The United States had no experience in fighting the kind of insurgency that was consuming South Vietnam internally. In this environment, there was little hope of developing a single, unified strategy to win, and little chance that Washington would have the stomach to implement such a policy, even if it was developed. So, while waiting for Washington to produce something that remotely resembled a real strategy, the military created new commands, kept the old ones, changed lines of communication, and debated the location of medical evacuation helicopters.

A few days after Temperelli's meeting with Colonel Merchant, he received word that his five Hueys had arrived at the Newport Dock in Saigon. Temperelli and Captain Bill Ballanger, one of the 57th's pilots, traveled to Saigon to pick up two of the helicopters. His plan was to send down crews later to pick up the remaining three.

The helicopters Temperelli and Ballanger were in Saigon to pick up were the only Hueys in country. They represented the very latest in helicopter technology and design. The lineage of the Huey could be traced to a 1955 Army competition to acquire a new utility helicopter with a turbine powered engine. The Korean war had taught the Army many valuable lessons and had turned up several glaring shortcomings regarding equipment. At the top of the deficiency list was helicopter lift capability. Among those companies in the competition was Bell Textron in Fort Worth, Texas. Bell's entry, the XH-40, beat out all other competitors. By today's standards, the developmental cycle was remarkably short and free of any major setbacks. Bell's prototype made its maiden flight in 1956, slightly ahead of schedule. One of the smartest things the Army did during the development of the Huey was to involve the Medical Corps in the design criteria and the selection process. In fact, the medical requirements received such emphasis that the competition was often referred to as the "ambulance helicopter" even though, in reality, the competitive process was to select an all purpose, utility helicopter capable of performing a wide variety of missions.

The XH-40 passed all qualification tests with flying colors, including the critical requirement of lifting an 800 pound load over a mission radius of 115 miles. After extensive testing and some modification, the Bell prototype was placed in production. The first production models, designated the HU-1, were delivered to the Army in 1959. In 1962, the designation was changed to UH-1A. Officially, the UH-1A was to be known as the Iroquois, following the Army practice of naming helicopters after Indian tribes.

However, Iroquois never caught on with the UH-1A. Since it was first designated the HU-1, it became known as the "HU-EE," and it stuck. Forever after, the UH-1 would be called the Huey, regardless of model. No one called it the Iroquois, and few knew, or even cared, that this was the official designation.

These initial production models were powered by a Lycoming T53-L-1A turbine engine capable of producing almost 800 horse power. What that meant to the Army in air lift capability was incredible. Each UH-1A was capable of lifting a maximum load of over 2,000 pounds. Maximum range was close to 160 miles and it had a top speed approaching 140 mph. Clearly, Bell had produced a winner with the UH-1A. It is only fitting that the first DUST OFF unit in country, the 57th, would go into the evacuation business with the first Huey, the UH-1A.

In Saigon, Temperelli and Ballanger were immediately confronted with the logistical problem of moving the Hueys up the coast. Nha Trang is over 200 miles northeast of Saigon, well beyond the range of the UH-1A under ideal circumstances. And there were no refueling points along the way. Clearly, some modifications were in order to increase the range of the UH-1A. Temperelli asked the logistical folks in Saigon if the cockpit heaters, useless in Vietnam, could be removed in order to accommodate additional fuel cells. His request was promptly denied on bureaucratic grounds—no one had been given approval to modify the UH-1As. However, Temperelli and Ballanger found a creative solution to this problem. They put a 55 gallon drum in the cargo bay of each of the Hueys, filled the drums with JP-4, and headed northeast toward Nha Trang.

Approximately half way to Nha Trang, they managed to raise the Special Forces camp on the coast at Song Mao on the radio, and received permission to land. With the assistance of the US advisors and the Montagnards they were advising, the drums were unloaded from the cargo bay and the Hueys were refueled with a manual pump. The helicopters drew considerable attention at Song Mao. The first UH-1As in country were being refueled, for the first time, with a hand pump at an isolated base camp. After thanking their temporary ground crew, Temperelli and Ballanger were airborne once again.

Almost immediately after lifting off from Song Mao, they encountered a strong head wind that began to eat their fuel at an alarming rate. Failure to make Nha Trang would force them to land on the coast and neither pilot wanted to make an emergency landing in what could be considered enemy territory. Determined to make Nha Trang, they pushed on through the head wind, hoping for the best. When the mountains to the south of Nha Trang came into view, both helicopters' fuel gauges registered zero. As they skimmed over the mountains, Temperelli requested immediate clearance to land from the Vietnamese tower operator.

Luckily, he received it. When they finally touched down at Nha Trang, the two helicopters had 7 gallons of fuel to spare. Now the 57th was almost ready to go to work as the first medical evacuation unit in Vietnam. There was, however, the matter of fuel that needed to be resolved.

When the other Hueys arrived a few days later, Temperelli was prepared to send two to Qui Nhon, a coastal settlement some 90 miles north of Nha Trang, as directed by the Support Command Commander, Colonel Merchant. However, there was no fuel for Temperelli's helicopters at Qui Nhon. To Temperelli's frustration, no one in Saigon seemed unduly concerned about the situation and his efforts to get Saigon to provide fuel at Qui Nhon were unsuccessful. Although logistics were a major factor, the problem also proved to be political. Temperelli learned that the Vietnamese government had to approve all fuel allocation and storage according to the orders of President Ngo Dinh Diem. As bad as this arrangement was, it was only part of the problem. The US Army had given the task of dispensing JP-4 fuel in the Nha Trang area to an Australian ESSO contractor. The contractor stored the JP-4 in 55 gallon drums about five miles outside the city of Nha Trang. The contractor refused to release fuel to the 57th without written authorization from the Saigon government. The US Army high command in Saigon allowed this incredible bureaucratic problem

Wounded Vietnamese farmers wait for medical evacuation after being injured by a booby-trap bomb in Binh Dung Province, northwest of Saigon. In the early years, before the arrival of American ground combat troops, Vietnamese civilians and soldiers were the principal users of the evacuation service.

to fester for days. So, in early May, Temperelli not only couldn't put two helicopters in Qui Nhon, he couldn't even get fuel at Nha Trang! During this fuelless period, a Vietnamese Air Force T-28 went down in the bay near Nha Trang. The 57th was helpless to assist. Also, a South Vietnamese Army unit was hit by an enemy ambush a few miles inland from Nha Trang. They had several wounded that needed evacuating, but the 57th could do nothing about it.

Finally, after a needless five day delay, the ESSO contractor received permission from the Vietnamese government to allow the 57th to draw fuel, fuel that had been paid for by the United States government. The fuel problem, however, was far from resolved. Since the ESSO contractor's site used no filtration equipment during any of its refueling operations, the 57th was forced to provide whatever filtration the fuel received. This became a tedious, time-consuming process. First, the fuel was picked up at the contractor's site in 55 gallon drums. The drums were then transported to the 57th's location at Nha Trang, where it was hand pumped into one of the 57th's 1200 gallon capacity M-49C storage tankers. The 57th had two of these. The M-49C had its own filter and water separator. After pumping their fuel through one of the tankers, Temperelli insisted that it be pumped into the second tanker for additional filtration before the fuel was put into the helicopters. This attention to detail on Temperelli's part was justified. JP-4 in tropical climates exhibits two characteristics which are both dangerous and hard to counter. A particularly nasty strain of microorganism flourishes in the hydrocarbon medium and clogs fuel filters, pumps and fuel lines. The second problem was condensation. Water tends to condense in fuel cells or tanks that are only partially filled. Condensation in a turbine engine can be lethal—it causes the engine to flame out. As a result, Temperelli refused to accept JP-4 from drums that were not completely full. This refusal did not go over well with the ESSO contractor and he threatened to terminate the 57th's fuel service. Temperelli called his bluff and the civilian contractor backed down. Temperelli was learning another valuable lesson about life in Vietnam in 1962—don't take any crap from people who aren't doing their job. Aside from the fact that the 57th won this round, it does illustrate one of the basic shortcomings of a US Army unit being dependent on a civilian contractor to logistically support tactical operations in a combat zone. Yet, incredibly, it was under these circumstances that the 57th went to work.

The first evacuation mission flown by the 57th came on the 12th of May. A US Army captain, working as an advisor to the South Vietnamese at Tuy Hoa, forty miles up the coast from Nha Trang, was in need of medical attention. The request, passed through Vietnamese channels, stated that the captain had a high fever. The mission was flown without incident and the patient was delivered to the 8th Field Hospital, where he was treated for gastroenteritis and dehydration.

Shortly after evacuating the captain, the 57th got another request. This time the call came through MAAG channels from a Vietnamese unit being ambushed near Cam Ranh Bay, about thirty minutes flying time to the south. Temperelli and Captain Don Naylor plotted the coordinates they had received and immediately flew to that location. The area on the ground appeared to agree with the area on the map. There was even smoke on the ground where, no doubt, the causalities were. Temperelli initiated an approach into what he assumed was a landing zone. However, as he came closer to the ground, he could clearly see that his landing zone was nothing more than a field being worked by a Vietnamese farmer and his water buffalo. The smoke was real enough, but it wasn't from a smoke grenade. It was from a brush fire. A very quick 180 degree turn and they were out of the area, climbing for altitude. A call back to Nha Trang confirmed what had happened—Temperelli and Naylor had been three thousand meters too far south.

With the new coordinates, they picked up their causality and flew him to the Vietnamese hospital at Nha Trang. While they made a successful evacuation, the 57th learned a very valuable lesson. During the time they were air evacuating their patient, who only had minor wounds, a far more seriously wounded soldier suffering from a fractured femur and internal hemorrhaging was transported by ground ambulance to the hospital. Clearly, communications would have to improve if the full potential of the 57th was to be realized.

As the 57th settled into the evacuation mission, the fuel problem continued to plague their efforts. In early July, Temperelli wrote a letter to the Support Group in Saigon outlining, in great detail, the problem his unit was facing in Nha Trang. He warned that unless serious measures were taken immediately to provide him with adequate filtration, increased maintenance down time, and possible damage or even loss of aircraft, would result.

Temperelli could not have been more prophetic. Barely two weeks after notifying Saigon of the potential for disaster, disaster struck. On July 22nd, one of the 57ths helicopters suffered an engine failure due to contaminated fuel. The pilot went through all the emergency procedures required under these circumstances, and executed a successful autorotation. However, at the end of the autorotation, the main rotor blade flexed down and severed the tail boom. Luckily, no one was injured because, by this time, the helicopter was on the ground. However, the aircraft was lost.

Temperelli's concerns could no longer be ignored by Saigon. Within a matter of days, a team of investigators arrived from Hawaii to inspect the fuel situation at Nha Trang. The team concluded what Temperelli already knew—the situation at Nha Trang was unacceptable and needed immediate corrective action. That's precisely what happened. A proper JP-4 dispensing station was set up at Nha Trang, under the control of Army petroleum storage specialists and held to the same high standards of other military fuel dispensing stations. Temperelli and the 57th were having an impact and getting a little respect in the process.

With the fuel problems finally solved, Temperelli could now operate effectively

The insignia of the 57th Medical Detachment. In time, all the DUST OFF units would adopt insignias of their own. However, many would use the 57th's as a model.

from both Nha Trang and Qui Nhon. Two Hueys were operating out of Qui Nhon. The Qui Nhon team had three pilots, two crew chiefs, two medics, a mechanic, a jeep and one of the fuel tankers. Through all of this adversity, the 57th had managed to maintain a high level of morale. Temperelli's efforts to establish the 57th as an integral part of the US mission was paying off. Most of this was achieved by the personal contacts he established with the people who could help him. He had gotten to know the Vietnamese Province Chief, Major Tak, very well. With the assistance of Major Tak and the MAAG advisors, Temperelli set up six designated evacuation sites in secure areas throughout the province. The 57th was doing everything possible to increase their efficiency in flying evacuation missions.

Still, the biggest obstacle was communications. People who needed to be evacuated could not reach the 57th. Requests for assistance had to relayed through various channels until the 57th was notified. Calls for evacuation were normally routed from an advisor through MAAG channels, which in turn were linked with Vietnamese military units throughout the province. Since Major Tak, the Province Chief, had communications with units throughout his province as well as the evacuation sites, the 57th used his assistance when possible for evacuation.

During the summer, an informal arrangement developed between the 57th and the Vietnamese military units. The 57th would take full advantage of the Vietnamese communication systems in evacuating wounded US advisors. In return, the 57th would also evacuate any wounded Vietnamese soldiers. This policy wasn't written; it was simply understood. Unfortunately, it wasn't understood in Saigon.

When the Support Command discovered that Temperelli was evacuating Vietnamese, he was given orders to stop it. Once again, Temperelli went to Saigon to take on the brass. He explained that without the Vietnamese communication channels, he and his unit would be virtually useless and that his efforts in evacuating wounded Vietnamese did not interfere with evacuating Americans. Since MACV had neglected to assign the 57th radio frequencies, Temperelli was forced to use communication channels assigned to the Vietnamese. In any event, he continued, he was not about to let a wounded soldier die if he could prevent it. Temperelli was so effective in explaining his vision of what an evacuation unit's mission should be that the Support Command revoked the directive. While the directive had been well intended, the reality of conditions in the field, far removed from Saigon, made it inoperative. From that meeting, part of the DUST OFF legacy was born. Never again would restrictions be placed on the kinds of causalities DUST OFF helicopters could carry. As the war progressed, soldiers of all nationalities were evacuated, including the enemy.

As the summer wore on, the 57th began to adjust to life in Vietnam. There were two pilots that needed to be checked out on the UH-1A and this was done. One bureaucratic hurdle after another was overcome, ranging from pay problems for the enlisted men to feeding arrangements for the unit. Those that weren't solved were simply ignored.

Saigon was a long way off, both geographically and emotionally. Temperelli had learned, the hard way, that not everything needed to be brought to the attention of the brass. Relations between the 8th Field Hospital and the 57th actually improved after a fairly rocky beginning. The only incident of note occurred shortly after the 57ths arrival when Temperelli asked if his men could eat in the 8th Field's mess hall. Temperelli's request was refused and the 57th had to subsist for over two weeks on the C rations they had brought from Ft. Meade. As it turned out, even this very deliberate snub from the commander of the 8th Field worked to the advantage of the 57th. As fate would have it, it was during this period that the 8th Field Hospital's mess hall was hit with a severe case of diarrhea. Some enlisted members of the 57th took great pleasure in pulling a juicy, greasy sausage out of a C ration can, wave it in front of an enlisted man from the 8th Field, and then exclaim, very loudly, "Man, this is really good,' then watch, with obvious glee as the victim of this prank made a mad dash for the latrine. In fact, during the great diarrhea outbreak, some members of the 8th Field came over to the 57th and dined on C rations that had been shipped all the way from Fort Meade. When the diarrhea problem cleared up, the 57th was invited to eat in the mess hall, finally making them members of the team.

Another issue that needed to be taken care of involved the living conditions. After living and sweating in the general purpose medium tents for almost two months, the men of the 57th decided it was time to improve their accommodations. Getting little help from the 8th Field, they hired a Vietnamese civilian carpenter and, after a very tough round of bargaining, the carpenter agreed to build a bamboo-framed building with a thatched roof and mat sides for the princely sum of $100. The new quarters were nearly 20 degrees cooler and considerably more comfortable than the tents. The fresh ocean breeze made the luxury of air conditioning unnecessary. It was just as well, since air conditioning was definitely unavailable. The crew at Qui Nhon actually had better living conditions than Temperelli and the rest of the 57th at Nha Trang. The guys at Qui Nhon moved into an old, French-styled wooden building with a tall roof and swing out windows. Also, the beautiful Vietnamese maid who cleaned and laundered for them did a lot to keep up their morale.

As the 57th gained more experience, they also encountered more problems. One of the difficulties encountered during these early days involved weather forecasts and updates. Actually, it was the lack of weather forecasts that gave the 57th's pilots a few exciting moments. In early July, the alert crew at Qui Nhon received an urgent evacuation request for a seriously wounded US advisor who had fallen into a punji trap. A punji trap is a wicked device consisting of sharpened bamboo stakes driven into the ground with the pointed ends sticking out. The idea is to have the victim step or fall on the stakes, creating instant casualties. It was late in the afternoon when the call came in and the dark skies to the west threatened rain, but Bill Ballinger and First Lieutenant Ernie Collins responded immediately to the emergency call. They flew down the coast and turned inland to the pick up point. The seriously wounded US advisor turned out to be a Vietnamese lieutenant suffering from a painful, but not serious, skin rash. Since they were already there, Ballinger and Collins picked up the lieutenant and headed back to Qui Nhon. The weather had been deteriorating since the mission started, but when they reached the coast on the return leg and headed north, it really turned ugly. The rain was now coming down in steady sheets, the wind was blowing, and it was dark. As if this wasn't bad enough, visibility was virtually non-existent. Ballinger contacted the Qui Nhon tower operator from about 20 miles south of the airfield and asked for a report on weather conditions in the Qui Nhon area. The operator, a US Air Force traffic controller, reported that the airfield had a 3,000 foot ceiling and five miles visibility. Surprised by this report, Ballinger assumed they were in an isolated weather cell he anticipated breaking out of shortly. However, after flying a few more miles and still not clearing the storm, Ballinger again radioed the tower and received the same report. By this time, the weather had deteriorated to the point where he and Collins could barely hover up the beach. Finally, they passed an area that Ballinger knew to be only five miles from the field. Once again, Ballinger contacted the tower and received the same report—3,000 foot ceiling, 5 miles visibility. Suspicious, Ballinger asked the tower operator for the source of the weather report.

"This is the official Saigon report for the Qui Nhon area, sir," the operator replied.

"Well, how about sticking your head outside and tell me what the hell you see!" Ballinger snapped, his suspicion now turning to frustration and anger. A few seconds later, the operator called back.

"Holy shit, sir!" the excited operator exclaimed. "You can't see a damned thing out there. You're in the middle of a storm!"

It took Ballinger and Collins thirty tense minutes to gingerly pick their way up the coast, hovering only a few feet off the sand. When they finally touched their skids on the runway and shut down the engine, they only had five minutes of fuel left. The 57th had learned another extremely valuable lesson—Saigon was definitely not the source of all knowledge.

In July, Temperelli and the 57th got a taste of how reporters would cover Vietnam in the coming years. It was during this period that the American news media first discovered Vietnam as a news source and made their first attempts to inform the American public about what was happening in this small republic half way around the world. Even then, most reporters working Vietnam allowed their zeal for sensationalism to carry beyond the limits of sound journalism. This tendency would continue to taint the press coverage until the war ended.

The reporter who visited the 57th was unremarkable from all outward appearances— short, balding, wearing glasses. He represented a newspaper in Los Angeles and had all the necessary credentials and clearances required to interview soldiers in the field. He even had a portable tape recorder and a couple of expensive cameras around his neck. He particularly wanted to talk to members of the 57th since the 57th was the only unit in Vietnam with the Huey, and also the only unit specifically dedicated to flying evacuation missions.

In the beginning, the interview went well. The reporter asked Temperelli what the unit was doing and Temperelli explained the area of operation, how many missions the unit had flown and generally how they functioned as an aerial evacuation unit. As the interview progressed, it became increasingly obvious that the reporter was not at all concerned with the facts. At several points in the interview, he encouraged Temperelli to exaggerate both the number of the wounded soldiers evacuated from the battlefield as well as the number of

To succeed in the high-risk business of flying DUST OFFs speed was just as important as skill, dedication, and courage. Getting airborne as quickly as possible was one of the highest priorities of the DUST OFF crews. Here, a crew races for their helicopter after receiving a call for help. As the war progressed it was not unusual for a helicopter to be in the air in under 3 minutes.

enemy contacts. Finally, in frustration, the reporter turned off the tape recorder and said to Temperelli, "Listen, what I really want you to say on the tape is that you and your unit have evacuated three hundred wounded."

"That's bullshit!" Temperelli replied. "We're not even close to that number."

"I know," the reporter conceded. "But my editors want volume. Big numbers sell papers. So why don't you just go along with it and let me punch the story up a little? I told the guys in Saigon that I wanted to do a favorable story and they liked the idea. Also, they gave me permission to fly on one of your helicopters and get some shots from the air. How about it, Captain?"

"How about getting the hell out of here before I choke you with that Goddamn tape recorder!" Temperelli exploded, bringing the interview to a rapid end and leaving the reporter in a state of shock.

This attempt at misrepresentation was all too common, both for the early years and during the years of full scale involvement. In 1962, however, the news media was obsessed with the evacuation pilots. Often, the media would depict them as flying all day, every day, with no break for rest or food. While it was true that during periods of intense fighting the DUST OFF crews spent many long hours in the air, there were also slack periods in which the pilots did little or no flying. The reality and complexity of Vietnam wasn't what the reporters wanted. What they wanted, at least in the early years, was a highly romanticized version of the war which depicted the pilots as larger than life figures. Later, as the war progressed, the reporters would drop this image in exchange for one far more negative and critical of American involvement in the war, which simply proves the oldest truism of combat —truth is always the first causality.

All of this caused Temperelli to offer this sage piece of advice to any reporter who might hope to write about the fighting in Vietnam. Temperelli believed there were three ways this could be done: 1. Don't come here at all. 2. Stay two weeks and leave. 3. Stay ten years before you write a word. Unfortunately, few reporters heeded this advice. The temptation to sensationalize was far too great to simply report the facts. Distorted and dishonest reporting was the second most destructive aspect to the war; only the enemy did more damage to our military.

As the 57th gained valuable experience in the Nha Trang area, one glaring weakness became increasingly apparent. The lack of reliable communications was severely restricting the unit from performing its mission. In late July, the detachment at Qui Nhon received an urgent request to evacuate a wounded American from a Special Forces camp twenty miles inland from Qui Nhon. In less than thirty minutes after receiving the call, a Huey was on the ground at the Special Forces base camp. Far from being happy at the sight of the helicopter, the commander of the Special Forces team was frustrated and angry. He had placed the call for assistance hours earlier. A trace of the call revealed that it had gone from the camp through the Special Forces regional headquarters, then to Saigon, then back north into Vietnamese civilian channels and finally to Qui Nhon. Fortunately, the wounded American recovered but the incident illustrated a very serious operational obstacle. Without an effective communication system that allowed those in need of the 57th's services to contact the unit directly, then there was no way for Temperelli's unit to perform at maximum efficiency. And, until the Army brass in Saigon assigned dedicated communication frequencies to the 57th, there appeared little hope that the picture would improve.

This situation soon produced a problem that could not be hidden or glossed over. By early July, the 57th had evacuated only 12 Americans and 40 Vietnamese. Clearly, these were not good numbers and Temperelli knew it. He also knew that the total blame for these poor numbers could not be attributed to poor communications.

In large measure, Temperelli's dismal numbers were the result of his location. The coastal area of central South Vietnam was not the best location for the 57th. Temperelli desperately wanted to increase the area of coverage and the simplest way to do this would be to move his unit inland, away from the coast. His desire had little to do with doctrine and everything to do with geography and math. By being on the coast, he was wasting exactly half of the operational radius of the UH-1As, since he was picking no one out of the South China Sea. In addition, most of the action was to the south of Nha Trang, around the Saigon area and further south, in the Delta region.

While this obvious fact was very clear to Temperelli, it had little impact on the senior military officers in Saigon. Several times Temperelli requested that his unit be relocated and each time he was turned down. At the time, Temperelli rationalized the inaction on the part of Saigon as a failure to understand how his unit could be best employed. In truth, there was a more sinister motivation at work in Saigon. Not everyone in Saigon endorsed the idea of an aviation unit dedicated solely to the evacuation of the wounded. This was a new concept endorsed by the Army's Medical Corps. However, all other Army aircraft in Vietnam belonged to the Transportation Corps. There were those in Saigon who believed that dedicating aircraft for the sole purpose of evacuating wounded soldiers was a poor use of valuable resources, particularly when those resources were the most modern helicopter in the Army's inventory. For those opposed to this concept, seeing the 57th fail was of critical importance. As a result, Temperelli's repeated request to move to a more fertile hunting ground fell on deaf ears.

To truly appreciate this philosophical battle, it is necessary to take a look at Army doctrine at the end of the Korean War. Then, the Theater Surgeon attached helicopter detachments to serve as air ambulances. When that war ended, these detachments had become bona fide medical units. Thus, the practice of having air ambulances under the control of the Medical Corps was established at the end of the Korean War and carried through the intervening ten years in doctrine and practice. These were ten years of peace and stability that did not require any doctrine to be tested in combat. While the logic and wisdom of maintaining this doctrine may appear obvious today, it was not obvious to the Army brass in Saigon in 1962. The quickest way to undo and change this doctrine was to allow the 57th to fail. If this happened, then all aviation units could be consolidated under the Transportation Corps and the evacuation of the wounded would become just another general support mission to be performed by any available aircraft.

To be fair, those opposed to dedicating helicopters to medical evacuation had a point. In combat, what is more important—getting troops into battle or getting the wounded off the battlefield? And, if it came down to making a choice, which choice should have the higher priority? The obvious answer would be that both are equally critical, but that response can be easily countered by the time-tested truth that nothing is obvious in combat, nothing is easy, nothing is certain, and damn little is fair. It was against this back drop that the real battle would be fought. What was at stake was the belief that the evacuation of wounded soldiers demanded the highest possible priority. As luck and fate would have it, the tiny 57th Medical Detachment would be thrust into the middle of this giant philosophical battle and it was not a battle the 57th could afford to lose.

Needless to say, under these tenuous circumstances, the 57th was in grave danger of losing its unique status as a flying ambulance unit. Temperelli, aware of some but not all the threats to the fledgling evacuation concept, had to be careful of all the bureaucratic minefields in Saigon. In essence, his mission became a high-wire balancing act as he pushed for approval to move his unit to a more productive area.

By late summer, the 57th had overcome more obstacles than any unit should have to face, ranging from living quarters to fuel. In fact, during these first few months, everything seemed to be a problem. It was only through sheer will power and dogged determination

that Temperelli and the 57th managed to maintain any degree of unit
integrity. However, as Temperelli
was soon to discover, things would
get a hell of a lot worse before they
got better.

Ironically, one of Temperelli's most serious problems was
caused by the new UH-1As. The
logistics system in country was not
geared to handling spare parts for
only five helicopters. This fact of
life forced the 57th to send requests
for spares directly to the US Army,
Okinawa. Sometimes the requests
were ignored. Often, they were
sent back because they did not
comply with logistical regulations
the 57th had never heard of. The
problem, however, was much
deeper than improper paperwork.
Okinawa stocked spares based on
20 flying hours per month per helicopter. The 57th far exceeded this
arbitrary figure, which meant that
parts were wearing out much faster
than Okinawa anticipated which,
in turn, meant that a massive back-
log was created, extending all the
way back to the states. Since there

When the 57th first arrived, policy forbade US evacuation helicopters from evacuating wounded Vietnamese. But Temperelli
and his men found the policy unworkable as he depended on
the Vietnamese for radio communication frequencies. In time
the policy was ignored and forgotten.

were no spare parts available, the 57th was forced to resort to a practice known as cannibal-
ization—taking parts from one helicopter and putting them on another—in order to operate.

In August, General Harkins, Commander of MACV, escorted General Earle Wheeler,
Army Chief of Staff, on a tour of Nha Trang. There, the Chief saw for himself two UH-1As
sitting forlornly on the flight line with no rotor blades on their masts. Wheeler assured
Temperelli that he would look into the matter and solve it for him, but nothing happened.
Even when presented to the highest level of the Army, Temperelli's problems persisted.

When other aviation units began receiving the Hueys in the fall of 1962, Temperelli
honestly thought his supply problems had been solved. Surely, he reasoned, spare parts
would now be available in Vietnam and he could get his dead-lined Hueys flying again.
Nothing could have been further from the truth. He soon discovered, to his horror, that the

combat aviation units were demanding what few remaining parts the 57th had. He was learning the hard way that being far removed from Saigon also had its disadvantages.

To make matters worse, stories were being spread about the low usage of the 57th's helicopters. Temperelli knew that if he couldn't increase the evacuations, his remaining three Hueys were in real danger of being cannibalized by the combat aviation units. And if he wasn't allowed to relocate, there wasn't much chance of flying more evacuations. He was, unfortunately, in the classic Catch 22 situation.

After festering throughout the early fall, the problem finally came to a head in November when the South Vietnamese Army planned a major operation into the Iron Triangle, a Viet Cong stronghold northwest of Saigon. Several of the new Hueys belonging to the combat aviation units that were scheduled to airlift the Vietnamese into combat had faulty starter generators. Temperelli received a call from the Aviation Officer in Saigon instructing him to remove the starter generators from all five of his Hueys and bring them to Saigon. When he objected to this request, it was upgraded to an order.

Under the circumstances, Temperelli had no choice but to remove the generators and take them to Saigon. However, he hoped to get an opportunity to make the powers in Saigon a counter-offer that would at least keep the 57th flying. With the generators outside in a borrowed jeep, he went to the office of Brigadier General Joseph W. Stilwell, Commander of the Army Support Group, Vietnam. Temperelli knew that Stilwell could overrule the Aviation Officer and allow him to keep the generators. Or he could make him hand them over. There was a third alternative and this was what Temperelli was counting on. He explained to Stilwell that taking his generators would leave South Vietnam without medical evacuation coverage, and since the impending battle would obviously create casualties, why not allow the 57th to come down and support the operation? It would also demonstrate the capacity of the 57th and, Temperelli hoped, lead to a permanent reassignment to either Saigon or the Delta.

The meeting lasted over an hour. Temperelli pleaded with the general to let him support the operation. In the end, Stilwell said no, and Temperelli surrendered the generators. The only thing Temperelli took from the meeting was a promise that his generators would be returned when the operation was over.

With the generators gone, the 57th was grounded from November 17th to December 15th. The only aviation unit in country with the sole mission of saving lives was shut down. This round had been clearly won by the operational forces, and medical evacuation had been forced to take a back seat.

For all practical purposes, the 57th was out of business during this period. This very well could have been the end of the story and, had the story ended here, the idea of helicopter ambulance units would have been little more than an obscure footnote to the Vietnam War. Fortunately, the story didn't end here because John Temperelli wouldn't let it end. Every day, he was on the phone to Saigon demanding that his generators be returned. He knew the longer he was grounded the harder it would be to make the 57th credible. It was simply a matter of time before the 57th became irrelevant.

It took a month, but he finally succeeded. On the 15th of December, one generator was returned and the 57th was back in business. With only one Huey, Temperelli did the best he could to provide evacuation coverage by flying back and forth between Nha Trang and Qui Nhon. The 57th limped and staggered through the remainder of 1962 in this condition. It wasn't much, but at least the 57th was still alive.

From one perspective, it had been a terrible year for the first medical helicopter unit in Vietnam. Medical evacuation as the sole mission of an aviation unit was sorely tested. For those opposed to the concept, there was reason to rejoice. They had very nearly managed to take the 57th out of action. However, the rejoicing was a bit premature. Fate had given the 57th a tough, tenacious, stubborn and extremely dedicated commander in the person of John Temperelli. He had taken everything the Viet Cong and Saigon had thrown at him and he still refused to quit. He was down to his last helicopter, but, by God, he was still in the game.

When viewed from this perspective, the fact that the 57th was still flying was a miracle. Considering all the obstacles placed in his way, Temperelli had performed magnificently.

The forces opposing him could have easily won and the noble experiment that was to become the brightest accomplishment of the US Army in Vietnam would not have happened. Unnoticed by almost everyone during these dark days at the end of 1962 was the unmistakable signs of a tradition slowly taking form. It would be called DUST OFF, and these two words would become the most famous radio call sign ever used in Vietnam.

However, DUST OFF became much more than a call sign; it became a symbol of hope, something to believe in when there wasn't much left. To the wounded soldier, DUST OFF was his salvation in the form of an olive drab Huey emblazoned with bright red crosses. Whatever else might fail him—and in this brutal, unforgiving war, much did—DUST OFF never would.

Temperelli could not have known then, but the battles he fought to retain the 57th as a unit dedicated to medical evacuation would have a profound impact as the war intensified. By keeping the 57th alive, Captain John Temperelli ultimately provided a service beyond measure to the tens of thousands of soldiers wounded in combat. But that was not his major concern at the time. All he wanted to do was his job as he saw it—evacuate the wounded. This simple obsession had cost him a whole series of clashes with the command structure in Saigon, which often viewed him as little more than an irritant.

Nothing had been easy for the young commander during this first year. Every time he challenged the powers in Saigon, he risked losing the 57th's unique status. Yet, he knew that if he did not fight, he and his unit would be slowly consumed by bureaucracy, indifference, and obsolete doctrine. As a direct result of his actions, none of this happened, and in a matter of months, the 57th would give birth to DUST OFF.

2

Hanging On
(1963: The Rules of Rescue)

arly in January, 1963, the 57th got a big boost from an unlikely source—the Viet Cong. Four hundred Army of Vietnam (ARVN) soldiers of the South Vietnamese 7th Infantry Division, accompanied by fifty US advisors, assaulted a Viet Cong stronghold in the Delta near the small village of Ap Bac. Ten CH-21 Shawnee helicopters, commonly referred to as The Flying Banana were used to fly the troops into combat. Four of these twin rotor helicopters were shot down. Also lost was a Huey flown by one of the aviation units supporting the assault. The Huey was promptly shot down attempting to rescue the crew of one of the downed CH-21s. On the ground, the battle was just as dismal. The ARVN soldiers failed to decisively engage the Viet Cong and, under the cover of darkness, the enemy faded into the night. Friendly causalities were high. Sixty-five ARVN soldiers and three American advisors died in the battle of Ap Bac, many of them bleeding to death while waiting for evacuation.

This action, more than any other single event, illustrated the case Temperelli had been making for moving the 57th closer to the fighting. While Saigon could ignore Temperelli, it was impossible to ignore what happened at Ap Bac. The reality of suffering needless causalities was finally making an impression on the command structure. On January 16th, barely a week after the battle, Temperelli was ordered to move his unit to Tan Son Nhut Air Force Base on the outskirts of Saigon.

While this was a step in the right direction, it wasn't a very big step. When Temperelli arrived in Saigon with his Nha Trang contingent, he discovered that no facilities had been made available to him. In a lot of ways, it was a re-run of his arrival in Nha Trang nine months earlier. Temperelli consulted the Support Group's logistics officer as to where he should set up. "Go find yourself a place," he was told dismissively. This proved to be easier said than done. Temperelli and his officers scoured the air base looking for a suitable location. When they found a place that would work, they were told they couldn't use it. When another area was located, they were told the same thing.

Finally, tired frustrated and more than a little pissed off, Temperelli simply claimed squatter's rights to a prime piece of real estate adjacent to a South Vietnamese Air Force unit and refused to move. The men of the 57th painted a sign that read, 57th MEDICAL

DETACHMENT—HELICOPTER AMBULANCE, stuck it in the ground in front of the hut that would become the Operations Building, and dared anyone to take it down. No one did. With that defiant act, the 57th had a place to call home in Saigon. Once again, the 57th was forced to take matters into their own hands and it paid off.

The next day, Temperelli called Captain Bob McWilliam, the officer in charge of the group at Qui Nhon and instructed him to fly the sole remaining UH-1A to Saigon. That flight, however, never took place. As McWilliam lifted off from the landing pad at Qui Nhon he experienced a tail rotor failure. Fortunately, no one was injured but that was the end of the original group of UH-1As Temperelli had brought with him. They had performed well considering they were the first version of a long and proud lineage of Hueys to see service in Vietnam.

Now, for the second time since arriving in country, the 57th was completely grounded, an aviation unit with nothing to fly. Temperelli immediately began lobbying the Support Command for new helicopters and within a few days of arriving in Saigon he was told he would be getting five new Hueys very soon. However, they would not be UH-1As. He would be getting the latest version of the Huey being produced by Bell in Fort Worth, Texas —the UH-1B. Until they arrived, the 57th was once again out of the evacuation business. The men spent the time they now had improving their area, making it more habitable in every way they could. They also made preparations for the helicopters' arrival. Knowing that the monsoon season would turn all unpaved or unprotected ground into a muddy bog, the 57th asked the engineers to pour a concrete pad behind the Operations Building to be

A DUST OFF approaches a Landing Zone near Pleiku.

used as a parking area. However, the engineers were engaged in a higher priority mission—they were pouring concrete to extend the runways at Tan Son Nhut. Undeterred by this set back, the men of the 57th "liberated" a large quantity of pierced steel planking (PSP) that had once served as a part of the runway. The engineers pouring the new runways had ripped it up and stacked it neatly in a storage area for use elsewhere. The 57th soon discovered this valuable stash and made plans to get it. After considering several alternatives, they finally settled on the direct approach. One of Temperelli's lieutenants bribed the Vietnamese soldiers guarding the PSP with three bottles of cognac and a carton of cigarettes. Within three days, the 57th had a first rate parking area large enough to accommodate all five helicopters when they arrived. It was this kind of creative problem solving that made the mission a lot easier to accomplish.

In many ways, this dead time was good. For the first time since the previous May, the 57th was together as a unit. The pilots flew with other aviation units in order to maintain their flying skills and when there was nothing else to do, the 57th explored the attractions of Saigon.

Saigon was far different than Nha Trang or Qui Nhon. It was a beautiful old city with wide boulevards and stately architecture. There was little question that this magnificent city richly deserved the title of Pearl of the Orient. The French influence was everywhere—French restaurants, cognac, French bread and no shortage of Citrons cruising the crowded, noisy streets. The Circle Sportive Club provided swimming and tennis and the Club Notice offered water skiing, rowing and motorboating. There was even a six lane bowling alley. It didn't take the 57th long to adjust to life in Saigon.

In February, while still waiting for the new Hueys, Temperelli turned command of the 57th over to Major Lloyd Spencer. It was a sad, solemn day for the men of the 57th. They were well aware of the fights Temperelli had waged on their behalf and loved and respected him for it. In an effort to show their appreciation, they had a party for him the night before he left. Temperelli had kept the unit alive during some very dark days; now it would be up to others to continue and build on what he had started.

On March 11th, the 57th was issued five brand new UH-1Bs, still on a ship in Newport Harbor. It took the men of the 57th only 12 days to get them ready and, on 23 March, the unit was operational once again. Things were beginning to look brighter. Not only would they soon be flying, they would be flying a greatly improved helicopter.

The engineers and designers at Bell had every reason to be proud of the UH-1B. Their objective was to build a better helicopter by improving on the UH-1A and they had succeeded. In all outward appearances, it looked almost identical to the UH-1A, but looks can be deceiving. Powered by the Lycoming 1,100 horse power T53-L-11 turbine engine, the UH-1B had greater lift than the UH-1A and considerably greater range. The UH-1B had an operational range of 260 miles and it could cover this distance in far less time than the UH-1A. In fact, one version of the UH-1B still holds the unofficial helicopter speed record of 222 miles per hour. The extra power of the UH-1B gave it a climb rate of 2,680 feet per minute, allowing it to quickly climb out of a hot landing zone. In addition, the UH-1B had

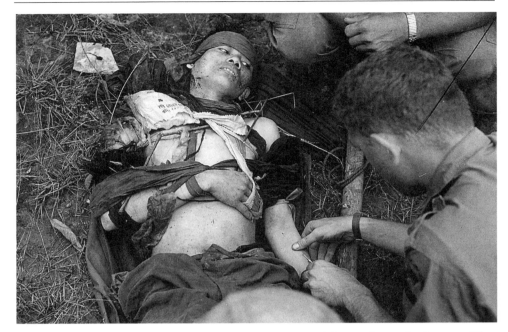

A Viet Cong soldier is prepared for evacuation. During the course of the war, thousands of enemy soldiers were flown from the battlefield by DUST OFF. This action took place in Quan Hodi An Province.

a larger cabin than it predecessor, giving it the capability of evacuating more wounded on each mission. This was a serious, "go to war" helicopter, fully capable of accomplishing great things in the hands of skilled, gutsy pilots. It didn't come any too soon, because great things was precisely what the 57th would demand from this magnificent bird in the coming months.

In early April, the good life in Saigon came to an end for some of the men of the 57th. Two of the new UH-1Bs were assigned to Pleiku, 75 miles northwest of Qui Nhon, in the rugged Annamite mountain chain. Several Special Forces teams were scattered among the Montagnard villages in this remote part of the country. It was mostly to support these American advisors that justified sending the two Hueys to Pleiku. Just two days after becoming operational at Pleiku, one of the new UH-1Bs was about to be put to the test by supporting a combat operation against a Viet Cong unit.

At first light, the Huey followed a flight of CH-21 Flying Bananas carrying South Vietnamese soldiers to the battle. As they approached the landing zone, Viet Cong gunners opened up with automatic weapons and shot down one of the CH-21s. The Huey from the 57th immediately landed beside the downed helicopter. The medic and co-pilot jumped out, under fire, and pulled seven wounded soldiers from the CH-21, including three American crewmen. Although receiving several rounds of enemy fire—including one round through the windshield—the Huey quickly lifted out of the combat area and flew the wounded to safety. Any questions about the UH-1B's capability soon dissipated in the early morning mist. It was missions such as this that began to spread the word throughout the remote areas of the country that, if you had wounded, the 57th would come.

As a result of moving two of his UH-1Bs north to Pleiku, Spencer had found a way to provide most of South Vietnam with some form of medical evacuation. South Vietnam was divided into four regions or Corps. Starting at the most northern end of the country, or I Corps, medical evacuation of wounded Americans was provided by the US Marines, who flew H-34 helicopters. Unlike the Army, the Marines had no equivalent to the 57th because their doctrine did not allow for an aviation unit to be dedicated to medical evacuation. The Marines doctrine was that any available helicopter could be pressed into service to perform an evacuation mission. As a result, evacuation of the wounded did not receive the same priority in I Corps as it was given in the Pleiku area but, in any event, the I Corps area was covered. With I Corps covered by the Marines, the two UH-1Bs stationed at Pleiku provided coverage for II Corps. Moving south, this allowed the three remaining UH-1Bs of the 57th stationed in Saigon to provide coverage of the two southern corps, III and IV. Now, all four of the corps or regions were covered with some form of medical evacuation. However, the coverage was spread dangerously thin, and each month the number of American military advisors steadily increased.

Another problem was becoming painfully obvious as the 57th expanded and improved medical evacuation. The reluctance of the Vietnamese Air Force to respond quickly and effectively to evacuation requests placed an added burden on the limited resources of the 57th. Although the number of Vietnamese soldiers wounded increased dramatically in 1963, the Vietnamese Air Force refused to establish its own medical evacuation capability.

Unlike the US Army, the South Vietnamese Army had no aviation assets. All Vietnamese aircraft belonged to the Vietnamese Air Force (VNAF), which was supposed to fly evacuation missions with any aircraft available. However, VNAF suffered from a lack of leadership and was plagued by poor organization. Whether a mission was flown or not depended as much on the mood of the pilot as anything else. Not only did VNAF lack a dedicated air ambulance unit, the US advisors working with VNAF indicated that it would be some time in the distant future before the Vietnamese could begin flying their own evacuation coverage. Rarely, if ever, did the Vietnamese commander of the aviation unit assigned the evacuation mission go along on the flight. If the decision was made to abort the flight, it was usually made by an inexperienced pilot lacking the necessary skill or maturity to make such decisions. A MACV report on this problem during 1963 stated:

"Usually the decision was made to abort , and the (Vietnamese) air mission commander could do nothing about it. When an aggressive pilot was in the lead ship, the aircraft came through, despite the enemy firing. American advisors reported that on two occasions only the first one or two helicopters landed; the rest hovered out of reach of the wounded who needed to get aboard."

Major Spencer, the new 57th commander, had been an instructor pilot in the H-34. Many of the other pilots of the 57th were H-34 qualified, also. They even volunteered to fly with the Vietnamese and train them on the finer points of flying evacuation missions. VNAF flatly refused. Although the Vietnamese had specially designated crews within their unit to fly evacuation missions on a day-to-day basis, they normally turned down the missions.

An American advisor in the Delta, reporting on a battle he had witnessed where several Vietnamese were wounded, wrote:

"It is common that, when (Vietnamese) casualties are sustained, the advance halts while awaiting evacuation. Either the reaction time for helicopter evacuation must be improved, or some plan must be made for troops in the battalion rear to provide security for the evacuation and care of casualties."

Fear contributed to this problem, but it was deeper than that. The problem stemmed, in large part, from a subtle class distinction between the Army of the Republic of Vietnam (ARVN) and the VNAF. Since the ARVN had no organic aviation units, they were at the mercy of VNAF when air evacuation was required. As a result, the VNAF had little organizational or emotional attachment to their sister service on the ground. By and large, the VNAF pilots were from wealthy, politically-connected families, while the average South Vietnamese soldier represented one of the poorest segments of society. No matter how you sliced it, the sad truth was this—in the final analysis, VNAF pilots could not be counted on to fly when they were needed.

Under these conditions, the MACV prohibition on US medical evacuation helicopters flying support missions for Vietnamese forces was routinely ignored. When VNAF refused to fly, the 57th picked up the slack. Such action on the part of the 57th was justified on purely humanitarian grounds. However, there were considerations other than humanitarian that made doing this a necessity. The American advisors throughout the country were learning what the advisor in the Delta already knew—the ARVN ground forces would not leave their wounded to pursue the enemy. Rather, they stayed in place to protect their casualties. Often, when the 57th arrived to evacuate the wounded, the Vietnamese commander on the ground would insist that the dead also be flown out.

While the 57th fought hard to give Vietnamese soldiers a high priority for evacuation, they could not guarantee that the wounded would receive first rate medical care upon arrival at a medical facility. Most of the Vietnamese military hospitals simply were not up to the task of handling a large number of casualties. Poorly staffed and administered hospitals, such as the infamous Cong Hoa Hospital in Saigon, were little more than glorified butcher shops. Relatively minor wounds often resulted in amputation or even death. All too often, wounded Vietnamese soldiers who had been rescued from the battlefield at great risk to the pilots and crew, died in the dirty corridors of the hospitals before even being seen by a doctor. This was one of the heart breaking realities that the 57th had to accept, yet they continued doing the best they could.

On more than one occasion, a pilot from the 57th would fly a severely wounded Vietnamese to an American medical facility in order to save his life. This was strictly forbidden by MACV regulations, but the resourceful pilots always managed to find a way around the rules, usually by claiming some mechanical malfunction which required them to land at the nearest facility. In cases such as this, the irony was inescapable. The pilots found it was necessary to save the patient twice—once from the battlefield and once again from certain death at the hands of overworked, often incompetent, Vietnamese surgeons.

As 1963 wore on, the number of US advisors grew. The 57th was flying many more missions than the year before, but had still not firmly established itself in the minds of the high command. In many ways, the 57th was still being treated as a bastard child—grudgingly acknowledged but not fully accepted.

The unit still had no tactical call sign that would clearly identify it to the troops on the ground, nor an assigned, dedicated communications frequency. As a result, the 57th had to improvise. For example, if a pilot was flying a helicopter with the tail number 62-12345, his call sign would be Army 12345. The unit conducted its internal communications on any unused frequency it could find. Most requests for evacuation continued to be passed through Vietnamese channels. Since the 57th had no way of knowing what frequency it would be using, it was impossible for the advisors on the ground to contact evacuation helicopters directly.

The valuable time lost in passing communications through Vietnamese channels was costly indeed. People were dying because there was no frequency or call sign assigned to the 57th. Major Spencer had brought this problem to the attention of the Support Command several times during March and April. He received no response. Finally, when his frustration level became unbearable, he decided to take more direct action.

A medic from the 1st Infantry Division gives a transfusion to a wounded soldier as he searches the sky for DUST OFF at Ben Cat, about 50 miles north of Saigon.

Spencer did a little checking and discovered that the Naval Support Activity in downtown Saigon was responsible for controlling and assigning all call signs and frequencies in Vietnam. Armed with this knowledge, Spencer decided to pay the Navy a visit. After explaining his problem to a sympathetic Navy officer, Spencer was shown a Signal Operations Instruction (SOI) book which identified all units by their call signs and frequencies. The classified document also contained a listing of all unused call signs.

"What would you like to be called?" the Navy officer asked Spencer. The question came as a shock.

"You mean I can pick my own call sign?" Spencer replied, surprised at the extremely helpful attitude exhibited by his new found friend.

"Yeah, why not? After all, it's your unit. I've marked the ones that nobody is using," the Navy officer told him.

Spencer carefully examined all the available call signs, trying to find one that would be appropriate for the mission of the 57th. Most of the selections, such as "Bandit," or "Gun Runner," seemed more fitting for the assault units. Then he came across one entry that caught his attention. It was "DUST OFF." He liked it immediately. When helicopters land, the prop wash from the main rotor blades blows dust on everything and everybody, particularly during the dry season. And, since Spencer's helicopters had to land to pick up patients, it seemed to fit his mission precisely. Plus, there was an added benefit that Spencer grasped immediately. Because it had an unusual ring to it, this was one call sign the advisors on the ground would not forget. His reasoning would prove to be one of the greatest understatements of all time. Spencer quickly scanned the rest of the listings in the book but it was only perfunctory. He had already made up his mind. When he left the Naval Support Activity, DUST OFF belonged to the 57th. Very soon, however, the 57th would belong to DUST OFF. All he wanted to do was give the 57th some identity and, hopefully, a little respect. He would be successful beyond his wildest expectations, but he didn't know it then. Quite by accident, he had given a name to what would become the most magnificent endeavor of the war. Others would give meaning to that name later on as the popularity and dependency on aerial medical evacuation grew.

It didn't take long for the word to spread that the advisors could now contact those beautiful birds with the big red crosses directly without going through complex and time consuming communications channels. At the same time, a strong association was made between evacuation and DUST OFF. In essence, they became the same thing in the minds of the men on the ground.

This led to a perfectly understandable mutiny of sorts in the late summer of 1963. In August, the National Security Agency, which had overall responsibility for communications security worldwide, decided to reassign the call signs of all units in Vietnam. There was nothing unusual about this. In fact, it was routine to periodically reassign and create new call signs in an effort to enhance communications security by confusing the enemy. DUST OFF was given to another aviation unit, the 118th Airmobile Company. However, an amazing thing happened. The 57th refused to give up their newfound identity and, even more remarkable, the 118th refused to use it, out of respect for the 57th. Despite lots of bureaucratic threats, neither unit budged. Something mystical was already growing around this call sign. Ultimately, the National Security Agency gave up and granted an exception. The mutiny succeeded. DUST OFF and the 57th remained one and the same.

By now, the markings on the DUST OFF helicopters had become standardized. There was a large red cross on a white background on both sides of the cabin. A small cross was painted on the nose bubble. Finally, the largest cross of all was on the belly or bottom of the helicopter, which was a source of comfort to the wounded soldiers waiting to be rescued. Seeing that huge red cross on DUST OFF as it settled into a hot landing zone was a great morale booster. The practice of placing red crosses on medical evacuation vehicles stretched back to World War I and even earlier. All of the Geneva Conventions ever held gave such vehicles a protected status during combat. The idea of the red crosses was to make them clearly visible and identifiable.

However, the Viet Cong had no intentions of honoring any such agreements. In fact, the red crosses were nothing more than aiming points for Viet Cong gunners. Captured enemy documents explained, in detail, how the gunners should aim their weapons in order to bring down helicopters. One document read, in part:

"1. The type (helicopter) used to carry troops is very large and looks like a worm (CH-21 Shawnee). It has two rotors and usually flies at an altitude from 200 meters to 300 meters. Lead it 1 times its length or 2/3 of its length when it flies horizontally. We will hit its head if we lead it 1 times its length and its body 2/3 of its length.

A stretcher crew hurries toward a waiting DUST OFF. With lives constantly hanging in the balance, time saved meant lives saved.

The distinctive red crosses that clearly identified these helicopters as flying ambulances provided no protection from enemy ground fire, The Viet Cong did not acknowledge the Geneva Convention or the notion that the wounded be allowed safe passage from the battlefield. For much of the war DUST OFFs flew unarmed, a fact reflected in their loss rate—three times greater than other helicopter units.

2. The type used to transport commanders and wounded looks like a ladle (UH-1B Huey). Lead this type aircraft 1 times its length when in flight. It is good to fire at the engine section when it is hovering or landing, or at the red crosses if it is picking up wounded. It is better to wait until the aircraft is full of wounded because it will be easier to shoot down."

Even when the DUST OFF pilots learned of the enemy's intentions, they refused to remove the crosses. It was more than simple identification. The men of the 57th were proud of what they were doing and the crosses were a very visible symbol that spoke volumes about their trade. The crosses would stay on, even if it meant additional risk. However, the issue of the crosses was not dead. It would come up one last time before it was resolved forever.

After repeatedly asking that his unit be given a mission statement, the Support Command finally complied in August with Spencer's request. With the publication of United States Army Support Command Vietnam (USASGV) Regulation 59-1, dated 12 August, 1963, the 57th became a legitimate organization, fully recognized by the command structure. While there was a lot of extraneous verbiage in this regulation, it all boiled down to what, specifically, was expected from the 57th. Finally, for the first time, the Army leadership in Vietnam gave the 57th specific directions and guidance concerning priority of evacuation. In descending order of priority, here is the way it was supposed to work: US military personnel; US military civilians; US government civilians; US private citizens; Republic of

Vietnam armed forces; and any others for humanitarian reasons. The MACV prohibition against evacuating Vietnamese soldiers was now officially dead.

Another issue that was settled in 1963 dealt with the number of pilots that would fly on each mission. While one pilot could, under ideal circumstances, fly the UH-1B, the DUST OFF crews soon discovered that a second pilot, or co-pilot, was far from a luxury. It was simply too much to expect of one pilot to operate the radio, read the map, and fly the helicopter, all at the same time. In addition, there was the very real threat that the pilot would be shot, thereby losing the aircraft, unless the co-pilot was sitting in the right seat, fully prepared to take the controls. As it turned out, requiring two pilots was one of the most sensible requirements imposed by the high command. There were countless incidents of helicopters landing safely after one of the pilots was seriously wounded.

DUST OFF's second year proved to be much more productive than the first. The number of US military personnel in South Vietnam rose to 16,300 during 1963, and DUST OFF flew 1,485 missions, evacuating almost 2,000 patients. Clearly, business was picking up.

As 1963 drew to a close, the 57th remained split between Saigon and Pleiku. However, it was becoming obvious that most of the action was in the Delta. This was where a majority of the fighting was taking place and where most of the causalities were coming from. The three helicopters in Saigon were doing the best they could to cover the two southern corps, but they were hard pressed to keep up with demand. On one day alone in September, 197 Vietnamese soldiers were evacuated from three separate locations near Ca Mau in the Delta. This large number of casualties was caused by the Viet Cong almost annihilating several hamlets in the area. The three DUST OFFs made repeated flights with Vietnamese jammed in the passenger compartments and standing on the landing skids. This mission put the UH-1Bs to the ultimate test and they passed. On one single flight, fourteen Vietnamese were flown to safety. Under these conditions, there was no room for the medic to provide any assistance to the wounded other than stopping the bleeding or administering morphine for pain. The last flight out was made after dark under heavy enemy fire. However, DUST OFF did not quit until all the wounded were lifted out. Although all three helicopters had bullet holes in them after this mission, they were all still flyable. So far, DUST OFF had been unbelievably lucky. No aircraft had been shot down, no crew member had been lost. This streak of luck would hold through 1963, creating an image in the minds of many advisors that the DUST OFF helicopters were truly blessed.

While the Americans and the South Vietnamese were battling the Viet Cong in the countryside, political developments were unfolding in 1963 that would dictate future US involvement in the ever-expanding war. The Kennedy administration still did not have a clear-cut policy on Vietnam. While the overall goal was to prevent a communist take-over of the country, there was no uniform agreement between Washington and Saigon on the best course of action to achieve this. In fact, there wasn't even agreement between Kennedy's advisors as to the best course to take. The major problem was that many of Kennedy's advisors did not grasp the true nature of this conflict. Thinking that they were dealing with a bunch of home grown, rag tag communists, they believed that the Viet Cong could be defeated in short order without a major commitment of American forces. What they failed to realize was that every action taken by the Viet Cong was being directed and supported from Hanoi with massive support from the Soviet Union and the Peoples Republic of China. In short, the Viet Cong were only the tip of a very large iceberg. This failure to fully grasp the scope of the communist insurgency in South Vietnam would continue to plague American planners for years to come.

To complicate matters even more, Kennedy and his top advisors were having considerable difficulty dealing with the leader of South Vietnam, President Ngo Dinh Diem, who had been elected President in 1956. Diem desperately needed American support, but was opposed to the ideas of American military forces directly engaged in the war. Although fiercely anti-Communist, Diem was extremely vain. In his mind, allowing the Americans to engage in direct combat with the enemy would make his forces appear weak. The fact that his military forces were, indeed, weak never seemed to penetrate his thought process. In many ways, Diem was an embarrassment to the Kennedy administration but since Diem was the president, there was little they could do about it.

Thus, while the US was promoting Diem as a hard working, dedicated fighter for democracy, Diem was actually acting like a feudal monarch. In reality, his public campaign against the communists had another, darker motive—to strengthen his own dictatorial power.

A wounded Vietnamese Marine is evacuated from War Zone D by an American DUST OFF unit. Often the wounded were carried to the landing zone in makeshift litters. Note the wounded soldier's boots tied to the litter pole.

A wounded US advisor is evacuated by the 57th at Dau Tieng, 40 kilometers northwest of Saigon. During the advisory years from 1960 to 1965, before US troops were directly involved in the conflict, thousands of American advisors were dispersed throughout Vietnam to advise district and province chiefs on defense, communications, and administration. The advisors were frequent targets for Viet Cong attacks.

As a Catholic, Diem's religious views were in the minority. He viewed the majority religion, Buddhism, as his enemy and tolerated no political opposition from this quarter. At a time when all of Diem's energy should have been directed at defeating the communist, who posed a fatal threat to democracy in South Vietnam, Diem began cracking down on the Buddhists, who hardly posed any threat to anybody. In protest to Diem's repressive regime, Buddhist monks began setting themselves ablaze in public. US television crews graphically captured these gruesome scenes and beamed them into American living rooms, causing Kennedy's support of Diem to come under serious attack at home. Under heavy pressure from the US, Diem agreed, on 16 June, to make peace with the Buddhists and put an end to religious persecutions.

However, Diem was not sincere. In August, Diem's brother, Nhu, ordered the South Vietnamese Special Forces to loot and ransack Buddhist pagodas in Hue, Saigon and other major cities. Over 1,400 Buddhists were arrested during this rampage, and Diem did nothing to stop it. Diem's misguided religious persecutions were rapidly eroding his support in several key areas of government. Opposition was growing in the military and was beginning to have a serious, negative impact on the war.

America had staked a great deal on Diem and Diem was not coming through. By late October, it was obvious that Diem could not last. America was being forced to look beyond Diem if the communist threat was to be defeated. General Maxwell D. Taylor, Chairman of the Joint Chiefs of Staff, had already prepared a list of key military units and commanders that could be counted on when the coup took place. South Vietnamese General Duong Van Minh would lead the forces that would overthrow Diem. It was no longer a question of whether Diem could survive; it was simply a question of when he had to be removed. Clearly, America had had enough of Diem.

The end came on 1 November, 1963, when the presidential palace came under attack from Minh's forces. Diem and his brother were forced to flee the palace and go into hiding in Cholon, the Chinese section of Saigon. The next day they were arrested and placed in an armored personnel carrier, where they were killed according to a prearranged plan of the military leadership, fully supported by the United States government.

Even though Diem contributed to his own demise, his death did complicate matters for the United States. It would now be impossible to continue the same low level of support for South Vietnam. While Kennedy had attempted to extend US influence and support democracy throughout Southeast Asia with a minimum of Americans, Diem's death changed this. Washington had been deeply involved in the elimination of Ngo Dinh Diem. There would have been no coup had the coup planners not been assured by the US that it was the proper thing to do. Like it or not, Washington would by involved in what followed. The Bay of Pigs fiasco was too fresh in the minds of Americans to allow Kennedy to retreat from another cold war commitment. Kennedy could not afford to lose his nerve again if he expected to win a second term in 1964. The United States was now riding the tiger. The only alternative left was to raise the stakes in South Vietnam and defend democracy there. It had now become a "must win" involvement with the details being worked out along the way.

Unfortunately, we will never know if Kennedy had either a win strategy or exit strategy for Vietnam. As a result, we will never know how committed he was to defending democracy there. He had precious little time to clearly assess the events he had placed in motion by allowing Diem to be eliminated. Barely three weeks after the death of Diem, Kennedy was assassinated in Dallas. Thus, in less than a month, both leaders of the two countries committed to containing communism in Southeast Asia were dead. Historians can only speculate as to what might have happened had they survived.

3

Major Charles L. Kelly
(The Man Who Was DUST OFF)

During times of crisis, it sometimes seems that fate arranges to place the right man at precisely the right place at precisely the right time. The fledgling DUST OFF operations desperately needed someone who had a single-minded obsession with medical evacuation. DUST OFF needed someone who was tough, stubborn, willing to take on the brass, promote the concept and, if possible, create a special attitude in the minds of the very special people chosen to fly the wounded from the battlefield. Such a man was about to make his presence known in South Vietnam and his actions would, more than those of any other person, assure the survival of DUST OFF. Major Charles L. Kelly was that man.

In a lot of ways, Kelly had spent his whole life preparing for this assignment. He was a small man, about five feet seven inches tall with a gruff, no-nonsense personality that almost hid a big heart of pure gold. By the time he arrived in Vietnam, he had already seen plenty of combat in both World War II and Korea. At the tender age of 16, Kelly ran away from home and joined the Army. Before the war in Europe ended, he saw action with the 30th Infantry Division. After the war, he enrolled in college and, under the GI Bill, earned a master's degree. In 1951, he accepted a commission as a 2nd Lieutenant and was assigned to the 11th Airborne Division in Korea. It was in Korea that Kelly fell in love with helicopters, recognizing immediately the potential these flying machines had as medical evacuation vehicles. In 1954, he went to flight school and earned his aviators wings.

The Georgia native was now in charge of the third generation of DUST OFF crews. Both Temperelli and Spencer had proven to be precisely the kind of commanders DUST OFF needed during their tenures. Temperelli fought to keep the unit intact during some very dark days and Spencer built on that by giving DUST OFF an identity, legitimacy and an expanded mission. Without the contributions of these two extremely dedicated commanders, there would be no story to tell. Now, it fell to Kelly to take DUST OFF to the next level and beyond.

Unlike Kelly, most of his pilots were fresh from flight school with limited flying experience. The policy of one year assignments was in effect in Vietnam, which meant that all the pilots that had flown for Temperelli and most of the ones that had flown for Spencer

Major Charles L. Kelly, the third Commander of the 57th Medical Detachment. More than anyone else, Kelly established the role of DUST OFF in Vietnam. In the process, he also established the DUST OFF legacy.

were gone. While most commanders would view this situation as a liability, Chuck Kelly actually saw it as an advantage. It gave him an opportunity to train them the way he wanted them to fly. There would be no painful unlearning to contend with. Kelly's pilots would not only be dedicated to flying evacuation missions—they would be obsessive.

One of Kelly's first priorities was to improve medical evacuation in the Delta. In early 1964, the Delta was the most hotly contested region of the country. This was where most of the fighting was taking place and Kelly immediately saw the need to have evacuation helicopters stationed there. Instead of having them fly from Saigon, pick up the wounded and then fly back to Saigon, Kelly wanted them stationed closer to the action. This would dramatically cut down on the response time which could very easily be translated into lives saved. His plan was to move the two helicopters that were stationed in Pleiku to the Delta. While such a move would leave II Corps without dedicated DUST OFF coverage, he felt that evacuations there could be covered with general utility aircraft until other DUST OFF units arrived in country. Kelly knew it was just a matter of time until more units like the 57th showed up in the combat zone.

It took a while before the Support Command agreed with Kelly, but his persistence paid off. On 1 March, Kelly's plan went into operation when the Support Command ordered the two Hueys supporting II Corps to be stationed in the Delta. The two helicopters and their five pilots, now designated Detachment A, 57th Medical Detachment (Helicopter Ambulance) Provisional, set up operations in the Delta at Soc Trang, approximately 60 miles southwest of Saigon. Soc Trang had been a fighter base for both the French and Japanese prior to the American's arrival. Soc Trang consisted of a compound about 3,000 feet long and 1,000 feet wide, surrounded on all sides by rice paddies. Detachment A shared the compound with the 121st Aviation Battalion, which provided maintenance support to the detachment's two helicopters. Chuck Kelly personally led the relocation to Soc Trang, leaving his Executive Officer in charge in Saigon. Actually, many of those close to Kelly suspected that he had actually planned it this way by taking advantage of a good, solid excuse to get out of Saigon and go south to the action.

However, before heading south to Soc Trang, Kelly made sure that the 57th was well taken care of. He had more experience in dealing with bureaucracy than his two predecessors, so it was fairly easy for him to manipulate the system to his advantage. Along with the relocation of the two Hueys from Pleiku to Soc Trang, Kelly insisted on a change in the command structure that controlled his unit. The new arrangement he negotiated with the Support Command had the 57th attached to the 145th Aviation Battalion for rations and quarters. Next, he managed to get the Support Command Surgeon to agree to provide medical supervision to the 57th. Finally, he had the unit placed under the MACV Joint Operations Center (JOC) for operational control. All of these were extremely clever—even brilliant—moves that diminished the control any single command could exercise over DUST OFF. Kelly's intent was to confuse and obscure the command structure, thus giving him greater freedom to perform the evacuation mission as he saw fit, free from interference from Saigon.

As the commander of the 57th, Kelly was not expected to spend much time in the Delta. Ostensibly, he was only there to set up Detachment A, after which time he would return to Saigon. He had even promised Captain Patrick H. Brady, one of the pilots than had been in Pleiku, that as soon as things were set up and running smoothly at Soc Trang, Brady could come to the Delta and relieve Kelly. In the meantime, Brady was flying evacuation missions out of Saigon, waiting for the call from Kelly telling him to come south. On one such mission, Brady was flying with Lieutenant Conway making a pick-up from a hot landing zone. The wounded were loaded aboard, under heavy fire, and Brady and Conway headed back to Saigon. However, just as they were clearing the trees at the edge of the landing zone, Conway took a round through the foot and had to be evacuated to the Philippines.

In addition to being a pilot, Conway had the additional duty of being the 57th's supply officer. When Kelly heard of the incident, he told Brady that he would have to assume Conway's duties as the supply officer since Brady had gotten Conway shot. Brady felt this was grossly unfair since he didn't deliberately get Conway shot and, besides, he hated the supply room. Brady's argument prevailed. Kelly finally relented and gave the young captain a firm date as to when he could take over Detachment A at Soc Trang. The date Kelly picked was the 1st of July. As fate would have it, 1 July would be a date few DUST OFF pilots would ever forget.

Kelly was soon proved right in insisting that the two helicopters be deployed in the Delta. The number of patients transported climbed from 193 in February to a staggering 416 in March. It was very hard to argue with this level of success. Very soon, Kelly and his crews at Soc Trang were burning up the Delta. Some of the pilots were flying over 100 hours a month. They quit logging at 140 hours for fear the flight surgeon would ground them.

It was during this period that Kelly began pioneering a new concept in medical evacuation—night missions. Recognizing the critical need to fly the wounded out of combat as soon as possible, it was apparent to Kelly that night flights would save lives. Almost a quarter of all evacuations flown during March were flown at night.

To facilitate their night missions in the Delta, the pilots constructed charts of the possible landing areas, outlining what few identifiable terrain features existed. Due to this kind of innovation, the 57th soon became the most experienced helicopter unit in Vietnam in conducting night operations. The Delta, which was level for the most part, was ideal for night operations. Flying at night was safer than day operations in one important respect; the Viet Cong could not see the helicopters.

A crew chief looks along the bank of a canal in the Mekong Delta for signs of enemy activity as his DUST OFF approaches a floating landing zone.

Unfortunately, the Viet Cong were not the only threat Kelly and his pilots faced in the Delta. Whenever DUST OFF crews flew close to the Cambodian border, they faced an entirely different threat—the Cambodian Air Force. In late 1963, the extremely unstable and unpredictable ruler of Cambodia, Prince Norodom Sihanonk, canceled all US economic and military aid to his country, and then promptly crawled in bed with the Soviet Union.

The Russians immediately provided Sihanonk with a number of MIG jet fighters and 27 anti-aircraft weapons. These MIGs and guns claimed several US and VNAF aircraft that happened to stray too close to the Cambodian border. It wasn't unusual for the Cambodians to conduct raids over South Vietnamese soil, simply looking for targets of opportunity. Thus, any mission flown to the western part of the Delta put the DUST OFF crews under additional risk. On one night mission near the border, Lieutenant Armond Simmons' Huey came under heavy fire from a friendly base camp. Simmons called the camp and identified himself as the DUST OFF they had requested and demanded an explanation. The camp's response was they thought Simmons was a Cambodian aircraft.

The Cambodian threat, as real as it was, never prevented Kelly or his pilots from flying any mission on the Cambodian border.

From all outward appearance, Kelly and his DUST OFFs were doing a magnificent job. Still, the issue of dedicating aircraft for the sole purpose of evacuating wounded was not settled. Incredibly, after two years of selfless service to the wounded, DUST OFF's very existence as a unique, self-contained medical evacuation unit was being questioned all over

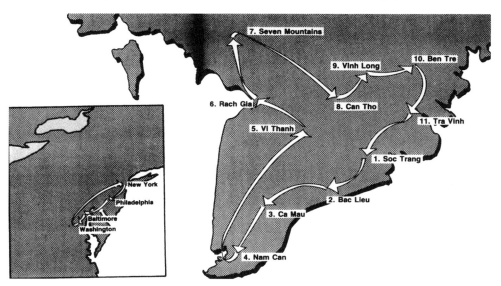

The map shows Maj. Kelly's nightly round-trip of the Delta. Kelly would routinely fly over 435 miles over hostile territory in search of casualties. The evacuation route took over three hours of flying time. If any of the locations had wounded, they would be loaded on board and the flight continued, unless the patient was critical. Then Kelly would fly to the nearest medical facility before resuming his circuit. The inset map shows the US equivalent of Kelly's nightly round-trip.

again. Some members of General Stilwell's staff were still grumbling about not having enough control over DUST OFF, and insisting that Kelly be brought under the control of the Transportation Corps. They were planning to take away Kelly's helicopters and place removable red crosses on other helicopters. In short, there was a movement afoot to make any available helicopter a DUST OFF.

The same old ghosts that Temperelli had successfully held at bay were coming back to haunt Kelly and the 57th. Spencer had given DUST OFF a name and even a formal mission statement, but apparently that wasn't enough to guarantee survival. The fact that Kelly was achieving tremendous success over a greatly expanded operational area apparently wasn't enough, either. There were still those who resented DUST OFF and they were influencing Stilwell to take away Kelly's helicopters. Part of the problem Kelly was running into was the inherit reluctance of the Army to change. All change, both good and bad, is resisted equally in the beginning. Since Kelly belonged to the medical corps, the more traditional combat arms elements of the Army viewed his growing influence as a threat. The fact that Kelly only wanted to support the combat elements of the Army seemed to be lost in the emotional reaction to his activities and the freedom of control he exhibited.

All the traditionalists could see was a very stubborn major who resisted all efforts to control him. In many ways, this criticism was justified. Chuck Kelly was a very stubborn, head-strong man. Of all the things he could be accused of, being diplomatic was not one of them. Kelly did not suffer fools or bureaucrats lightly. He had seen too much of combat and needless death to believe anything other than his instincts. And his instincts told him to fight for this revolutionary concept called DUST OFF. If it rubbed the hierarchy in Saigon the wrong way, then that was just too damn bad in Kelly's view. He was not intimidated by rules, regulations and policy drawn up far form the battlefield. As far as Kelly was concerned, he was making policy with each mission, and it was up to the hierarchy to write it down, refine it, and hold it close. And he was certainly not bashful about making his views known in meetings he was called to attend in Saigon. To his credit, Kelly told the same story in the great halls of Saigon that he told to the troops in the paddies of Soc Trang. The clashes he and General Stilwell engaged in during these meetings became legendary.

Returning from one such meeting with Stilwell, Kelly called his pilots together and said, referring to Stilwell, "That man is not our friend." He told them that DUST OFF was in for the fight of its life—the unit had to prove its value beyond a shadow of a doubt. Up to this point, the 57th had quickly responded to any and all calls for assistance. Now, under the very real threat of being disbanded, Kelly actually went looking for business. Night missions were no longer unusual—they were routine. Kelly immediately started a pattern of flying almost every night, usually taking a different co-pilot with him on each mission. His objective was nothing short of monumental—Kelly was hell bound and determined to prove that he could cover the Delta, all 12,000 square miles of paddies, swamps, forests and mountains.

On a typical night mission, Kelly and his crew would lift off from Soc Trang at about dusk and head southwest for the marshes of Bac Lieu, home for two signal units and a team from the 173rd Aviation Company. From Bac Lieu, Kelly's DUST OFF would head south to Ca Mau, one of the original strongholds of the Viet Minh, the forerunners of the Viet Cong. After leaving the forested swamps of Ca Mau, Kelly would fly south to Nam Can located at the very southern tip of South Vietnam. At Nam Can, Kelly would turn and fly north to an area called Seven Canals. After a check for casualties at Vi Thanh, Kelly would head northwest to Rach Gia on the Gulf of Siam. From there, he would shoot a course to the Seven Mountains region, right on the Cambodian border, totally disregarding the Cambodian anti-aircraft threat. From Seven Mountains he would fly southeast to Can Tho where 14 small American units were stationed, then northeast to Vinh Long on the Mekong River. From there, the course was due east to Ben Tre, south to Tra Vinh with a handful of US advisors, and, finally, home to Soc Trang.

Each night, Kelly would encounter different categories of patients—wounded American advisors, wounded ARVN soldiers, seriously injured women and children victimized by Viet Cong attacks on hamlets and market places, snake bite victims, accidents, and every other possible combination of casualties. It really didn't make much difference to Kelly. If any of these locations had patients, they were loaded aboard and the flight continued, unless the injury required immediate attention. In that event, the patient would be flown immediately to the nearest medical facility and the circuit would continue. This nightly route covered over 700 kilometers and took more than three hours to fly. On many nights, Kelly would carry 10 to 15 patients. Without question, many would have died without a night evacuation.

One American advisor in the Delta, Captain Don Masters, described a typical Kelly night mission this way, from his unique perspective on the ground:

"It was nearing midnight. A lonely figure sat in the semi-darkness keeping a night vigil. The radio nearby was silent, except for the static from the squelch that chattered softly. Outside, the sky was clear. There was no moon, but the stars glittered brightly. And then, from the distance, came the faint sound of a helicopter. As the sound grew louder, the man in the hut moved over to the window and peered out. He tried to spot the UH-1B he knew was coming closer. But he looked in vain, and he knew why. If he was right, the ship would be flying without lights. The radio static was broken by a southern Georgia drawl."

"Bayonet Two, this is ole DUST OFF. Over."

"This is Bayonet Two," the man in the hut answered.

"This is DUST OFF. Just passing over. Everything okay?"

"This is Bayonet Two. All's quiet, thank you."

"Okay. Take er easy, now. DUST OFF out."

This simple, yet eloquent tribute to DUST OFF speaks volumes for the positive effect Kelly was having on the advisors scattered throughout the Delta. Captain Masters' words expressed the feelings of all those Americans fighting for South Vietnam's freedom in the endless tracts of swamps, rice paddies and forests that made up the dangerous, yet lonely, stretches of the Delta. This was not simply idle, late night, radio chatter DUST OFF and Bayonet were engaged in. It was a very real, critical link in the life line that gave the Americans on the ground reason to believe they were not completely on their own. These links needed to be reestablished and renewed as often as possible. Advisors such as Masters knew the value of these brief nightly conversations with Kelly and eagerly awaited his nightly rounds. They needed him even when they had no wounded. There was something very reassuring about knowing DUST OFF was out there and that DUST OFF would come when all hell broke loose.

In April alone, the unit flew 113 hours at night, evacuating over 100 patients. Kelly was assisted on these nightly missions by the US Air Force, which maintained a very sophisticated aerial surveillance radar site at Can Tho. By keeping in touch with the radar operators, Kelly knew where he was during the long, nightly flights criss-crossing the Delta. By telling them his destinations, the Air Force knew where he should be and, if necessary, give him course corrections. This radar site, known as "Paddy Control," provided invaluable assistance in the Delta, which had few natural terrain features to follow under ideal flying conditions during the day. At night, the Delta was even more difficult to fly.

It was a great comfort to the DUST OFF crew to know that their lonely missions were being watched on a radar screen at Can Tho. However, Paddy Control did a lot more than provide navigational assistance. Messages were relayed through Paddy Control on the number of patients picked up and their condition. Paddy Control, in turn, would notify the American

A night evacuation mission in the Delta flown by the 57th's 1st Lt. Armand Simmons early in 1964. Night missions were a new concept pioneered by Kelly, who was eager to fly the wounded out of combat as fast as possible. One of the aids that made night flying more comfortable was the AN/APX-44 transponder installed in the 57th's helicopters. This device made it possible for Air Force radar stations to positively identify the DUST OFF helicopters and vector them to and from a pick-up site.

and Vietnamese hospitals in order to prepare the hospitals for the inbound wounded. In addition, Paddy Control would pass on the latest weather information, making it possible for DUST OFF to avoid thunderstorms, squalls and other adverse weather conditions. Every night, as part of the ritual, Kelly would land at Can Tho and he and the crew would visit a few minutes with the Paddy Control technicians, have a cup of coffee, then get back on the circuit.

It was apparent to anyone who spent any time with Kelly during this period that he loved the Delta. He was perfectly content to leave the day-to-day problems of command with his executive officer, Captain Paul Bloomquist, back in Saigon. Kelly had no love or time for paperwork. He would go to Saigon when it was absolutely necessary to sign some form or document, or attend one of Stilwell's meetings, but he didn't like to. Whatever he was supposed to sign had better be right when he got there or he would raise hell. His officers back at Saigon tried to coordinate all the administrative details to coincide with Kelly's meetings with Stilwell, thus saving their boss a needless trip. It didn't always happen that way, so Kelly made many more trips to Saigon than he wanted to.

While he may not have been a stickler on administrative procedure and paperwork, he was absolutely demanding when it came to instilling his own unique attitude in the young DUST OFF pilots. Kelly led the only way he knew how—by example. One of the pilots who flew with him put it this way:

"He (Kelly) put his ass on the same block with everybody else—it was there for anyone to slice. We all admired and respected that. He had balls."

Kelly's rule on refusing missions was simple—you did not refuse to fly a mission. This rule led to the most important and sacred rule of all—the wounded always came first. Kelly let nothing stand between DUST OFF and the men who needed it. Absolutely nothing stopped him. It was this obsession that earned Kelly several nicknames, including "The Mad Man," and "Crazy Kelly." Frequently, he would nurse a severely wounded Huey home, full of holes, smoking and spurting fuel, threatening to quit flying at any moment. Yet he always made it back. Those that knew him best said Kelly flew more by sheer guts and determination than finesse or technique.

On one mission in late May, enemy ground fire forced Kelly away from the landing zone before he could get the wounded. Within minutes, he attempted the same approach in exactly the same manner. This time he succeeded, despite withering enemy fire. While the medic and crew chief loaded patients, Kelly got out of the cockpit, with the engine running, and sprayed the enemy's position with a Thompson submachine gun. With the loading complete, Kelly jumped back in the cockpit and prepared for lift off. However, before he cleared the landing zone, the DUST OFF took several hits. One round shattered the windshield, showering Kelly and the co-pilot with plexi-glass. Another round hit the main fuel valve. This should have shut the Huey down but it didn't. Still under fire and spewing fuel at an alarming rate, Kelly flew out with the wounded. Approaching Soc Trang, he radioed the control tower that he had very little fuel left, and asked if he could have priority on landing. No problem, the tower replied. They were used to such requests from Kelly.

"Anything else, sir?" the tower operator asked.

"Yes," Kelly answered. "How about some ice cream? It's a little hot."

Just as the skids of the bullet-riddled DUST OFF touched the tarmac, the engine quit. As the rotors were winding down, the base commander drove up with a quart of vanilla ice cream and handed it to Kelly through the shattered windshield. Later, the maintenance crew counted over thirty hits in the Huey, and the fuel tanks were dry. They could not explain how Kelly made it home, but he did.

It was incidents such as this that served as the foundation for the Kelly legend. However, as important as these episodes of personal courage were, they were no more important than Kelly's goal of instilling the right attitude in the men of the 57th. In fact, the pilots tried to keep him from flying many of the missions he flew for fear they would lose him. They were far more comfortable when Kelly was raising hell with Saigon than they were when he was getting shot up over the Delta.

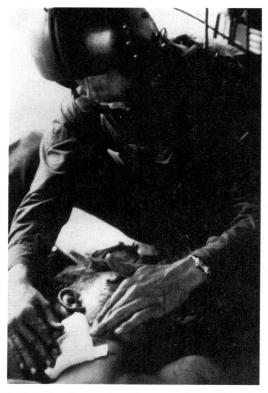

Applying bandages and comforst was all part of the airborne medic's job. Nothing was more soothing to the wounded than knowing that they were in competent hands. Cool and calm under fire, DUST OFF medics were as critical to the success of an evacuation mission as the pilot.

It wasn't long before Kelly was battling with Saigon over a new issue. He continued with his indoctrination of his pilots while becoming embroiled in a political fight with the Army's Surgeon General's office. As a medical unit, the 57th actually belonged to the Surgeon General. Kelly belonged to the Medical Service Corps (MSC). Officers in the MSC supported the Medical Corps (MC), which was composed of doctors, nurses and other medical professionals. Kelly had made it clear when he assumed command that he felt flying medical evacuation helicopters should only be performed by Medical Service Corps officers. In fact, Kelly believed that flying such missions should be the highest priority of MSC pilots. In Kelly's view, there was no higher priority. However, Kelly's strong feelings on this matter differed sharply with the views of the Surgeon General's Aviation Branch.

Sitting in Washington, far removed from combat, the aviation branch naively believed that MSC officers could get more combat experience flying with combat aviation units than flying with DUST OFF. This was not true and Kelly knew it. However, Kelly had a far more pressing reason for countering this faulty thinking—the very survival of DUST OFF. Without a reliable source of pilots, the concept would fail, and he knew it. If his own branch, the Surgeon General, failed to grasp this basic truth, then DUST OFF would not survive. If MSC pilots were sent to units other than the 57th in the mistaken belief that they would get more combat experience, Kelly knew he would have difficulty finding enough qualified pilots to stay operational. In short, if Kelly did not get strong support from his own kind, the medical corps, he could hardly expect anyone else to come to his defense. In a bizarre sort of way, Kelly was fighting a battle on all fronts of the US Army to keep DUST OFF alive. So far, he had succeeded on sheer guts, determination and audacity.

While this situation was personally frustrating, Kelly believed he could change the thinking of the Surgeon General's office by explaining exactly what was happening in the Delta. He wrote several letters, asking that someone visit the 57th for a first-hand look at what was happening. Kelly honestly believed that if senior medical officers saw the kind of operation he was running, he would be given more support, and possibly other units such as the 57th would quickly be deployed. Unlike the Army's leadership in Saigon and Washington who believed the war in Vietnam would be over quickly, Kelly knew they were in for a long haul and needed to prepare for it.

"As for combat experience," he wrote to the Surgeon General, "the pilots in this unit are getting as much or more combat flying experience than any unit over here. I fully realize that I do not know much about the big program, but our job is the evacuation of casualties

A doorgunner scans the terrain for any sign of Charlie as his ship eases into the landing zone. Due to the high loss rate of DUST OFFs this kind of prudent self-defense became a necessity. Often, DUST OFFs had to shoot their way out of hot LZs.

This photograph graphically illustrates the hazards of flying DUST OFFs. Landing zones, many of them hastily hacked out of triple-canopy jungle, were often a tight squeeze, with barely enough room for the rotor blades to clear the trees.

from the battlefield. This we are doing day and night, without escort aircraft, and with only one ship per mission. The other units fly in groups, rarely at night, and always heavily armed."

No one ever came to take a look at Kelly's operation, but he continued writing letters. He also continued to train his pilots in all aspects of flying in a combat zone, including the art of tactical flying. By studying the terrain, the pilot could often find a secret key, or safe route, into the landing zone. It was very important to note such things as the height of the elephant grass and rice dikes, and the width of trails, rivers and canals. Wind direction and speed were also critical factors. Often, by paying close attention to all these details, it was possible to avoid likely ambush sites.

However, as good as the DUST OFF pilots were getting at flying under all conditions and every conceivable situation, another very real problem was developing. By the spring of 1964, the UH-1Bs were over a year old and were showing signs of wear. The maintenance crews did a remarkable job of patching up bullet holes and keeping the Hueys in the air, but there was nothing they could do to offset the incredible number of hours on the

Scenes like this were played out thousands of times during the Vietnam War. A medical evacuation helicopter settles into a landing zone and for this wounded soldier, the war is over. Note the prop wash blowing down the grass. It was one of the reasons why the call sign DUST OFF was so appropriate, and why it lasted throughout the war.

engines, transmissions and airframes. No one ever expected these helicopters to fly the hours they were flying and there was no way to reduce these hours. While the pilots could fudge the log books and stop logging hours at 140 per month, there was no way to disguise the toll these hours were taking on the Hueys. Yet the missions had to be flown. Now, in addition to the constant risk of being shot down, the crews were contending with the very real possibility that, on any given mission, their aircraft would simply quit flying.

And, on top of everything else, communications continued to be a constant problem. Sometimes the request for DUST OFF would come within minutes of an incident; other times it would take hours. On occasion, the people calling for DUST OFF had moved on by the time the helicopter arrived, or the wounded had died. Even when DUST OFF had direct communication with the unit on the ground, there was always the risk that the Viet Cong would be waiting to ambush the evacuation helicopter. The Viet Cong knew that if there were wounded on the ground, help would arrive eventually. They knew that, sooner or later, the helicopters with the big red crosses would be overhead. All they had to do was wait. Kelly and his pilots were well aware of this, yet they always flew the mission. Both the Viet Cong and the friendlies on the ground could count on it.

Late on the afternoon of 11 April, Kelly received a mission request to evacuate two wounded Vietnamese soldiers from the Co To Mountains, part of the Seven Mountains region of An Giang Province. While most of DUST OFF's missions in the Delta were over flat, marshy terrain, they occasionally had to work the difficult, mountainous area near the Cambodian border. This happened to be one of those times.

When he arrived on the scene, Kelly discovered that the only landing zone near the troops was a small area, barely 25 meters square, right on the side of the mountain. The landing zone, if it could be called that, was surrounded on all sides by trees. Higher up the mountain, above the trees, were the Viet Cong, patiently waiting for Kelly.

From at altitude of 500 feet, it looked damn near hopeless. To avoid hitting the trees, Kelly would have to lower the Huey straight down, exposing the helicopter to enemy fire in the process. As bad as it looked, Kelly decided to give it a shot. Despite the updrafts common to mountain flying, the mists, and the rapidly approaching darkness, Kelly shot an approach to the tiny clearing. The enemy opened fire and kept firing until the ship disappeared below the treetops. Due to the steep slope of the clearing, Kelly could not actually land; he was forced to set the aircraft down very gently on one skid while one of the patients was loaded aboard. However, the other wounded soldier was still being carried up the mountain.

Kelly was in a very tough position. If he hovered above the clearing, the VC would have a very easy target; if he sat there with only one skid on the ground, he ran a strong risk of being hit with a sudden updraft that could slam him into the side of the mountain or flip him over. The third option—flying out with only one of the wounded—never entered his mind. Since the patients always came first, Kelly sat there, precariously balancing the ship on one skid, for over 20 agonizing minutes.

Finally, with both casualties on board, Kelly gently pulled away from the mountain and climbed straight up above the trees, exposing himself once again to the VC gunners. As they opened with an intense barrage, Kelly's medic began working on the wounded, unfazed by the rounds streaking past the Huey. Fortunately, the enemy gunners were having a bad day. Perhaps it was due to the gathering darkness combined with the mist. For whatever reason, the mission was successful. Kelly had put his ass on the block once again and they had failed to slice it. One of the wounded had been hit five times. Both survived, thanks to DUST OFF and Kelly.

4

A Tradition is Born
(1 July, 1964)

While there was nothing Kelly could do about taking enemy fire in the air, he would try, at every opportunity, to even the odds when he was on the ground. The helicopters were most vulnerable when they were in the landing zones, taking on patients. This was where the VC wanted to catch a DUST OFF, preferably with members of the crew outside the helicopter loading wounded. It was during times such as this that Kelly started the rather unorthodox practice of hopping out of the cockpit and shooting at the enemy. Soon, other DUST OFF pilots started doing the same thing. Kelly viewed such action as being in the "patients' best interest."

Concern for the patient was the single most important factor that drove Kelly. If, in his opinion, there was a rule or regulation that prevented him from doing all he could for the wounded, he simply ignored the rule. "After all," he once remarked, "it's a big country and one little unit commander down in the Delta is hard to find." This kind of philosophy was being ingrained in Kelly's pilots who, like their boss, made decisions based on the situation and their own good judgment. Often, the DUST OFF crews found themselves creating policy on the spot, since no existing rule or regulation covered the specific situation at hand.

For example, on one occasion, Captain Pat Brady was asked by a US advisor if he would fly a load of ammunition to a unit in desperate need of it. The advisor saw no reason why Brady shouldn't honor his request since Brady was going that way anyway to pick up some wounded Vietnamese. "We're all in this together," the advisor reasoned. "If it makes you feel better, consider the ammo preventative medicine." While Brady had some reservations about the propriety of such a request, he did it. The reasoning of the advisor had been compelling. Later, when Kelly found out, he questioned Brady. Explaining his actions, Brady told his boss what the advisor had said.

"Do you think ammo is preventative medicine?" Kelly asked.

"I do, Brady replied." Kelly considered this answer for a moment and smiled. He liked Brady. In many ways, Brady was a younger version of Kelly. Plus, it was the kind of answer Kelly himself would have given had someone questioned his actions.

"Then, by God, that's what it is," Kelly said, officially certifying ammunition as the very best form of preventative medicine. After that, none of the pilots hesitated to carry food, water, rice, mail, beer or anything else that would provide a service, so long as it did not interfere with the primary mission of the 57th.

In late June, Kelly's old adversary, General Stilwell, was making arrangements to leave Vietnam. His replacement as Support Command Commander, Major General Delk Oden, had arrived in May. As part of the departing ritual, Stilwell traveled throughout the country to say good-bye to the various units that made up the Support Command. In this regard, the 57th was no different. Stilwell arrived at Soc Trang on the 27th of June. The fate of the 57th was far from settled and Stilwell's attempts to take away the unit's helicopters were still fresh in everyone's mind. Under these difficult circumstances and given the personalities of these two men, it could have been an extremely tense, awkward affair.

However, Kelly demonstrated his unique ability to defuse a potentially explosive situation with an irreverent sense of humor. At the farewell ceremony, after General Stilwell made some appropriate remarks regarding the contributions of the 57th, Kelly presented Stilwell with a walnut plaque bearing five metal red crosses. On each cross was a tail number that corresponded to one of the unit's helicopters. As Stilwell accepted the plaque, Kelly remarked, loud enough for everyone present to hear, "Here, General. You wanted my goddamned helicopters, you can have them! Take them home with you!"

The scene was pure, vintage Kelly. It was bold, audacious, and the troops loved it. The general smiled graciously as he accepted the gift and then laughed out loud as the full impact of what Kelly had done began to sink in. Only Chuck Kelly could have gotten away with this stunt. Only Kelly could reduce the crusty old general to laughter over an emotional issue they had clashed on so often during the past few months. At Soc Trang, on the 27th of June, Kelly and Stilwell bid each other farewell with each man retaining profound respect for the other.

July 1st started out as another routine day for the 57th, providing any day during this tumultuous period could honestly be called routine. A request for DUST OFF came in from a unit in contact with the enemy near Vinh Long. While other pilots were ready to go, Kelly decided he would fly the mission and he selected Captain Dick Anderson to be his co-pilot. An American sergeant accompanying the Vietnamese unit had been wounded in the leg by a mortar round. There were wounded Vietnamese as well. On this mission, Kelly had an Army doctor with him. It had been the practice, whenever possible, to carry a doctor when there were American casualties on the ground. Kelly and Anderson flew immediately to the area and established radio contact with the unit on the ground, which had the call sign Dragonfly Bravo. Kelly asked Dragonfly Bravo to mark his position with smoke. When this was done, Kelly made his approach. The enemy fire was intense. As Kelly hovered near the ground searching for the casualties, the VC focused all their fire on the DUST OFF. Due to the heavy fire and the closeness of the enemy, the South Vietnamese and their US advisors were staying low.

"Dragonfly this is DUST OFF. Where are your wounded?" Kelly demanded. Clearly, this landing zone was not even contested; the enemy owned it outright.

"DUST OFF, this is Dragonfly. Back off! There's too much fire!" Dragonfly replied desperately. "Get out!"

"When I have your wounded," Kelly answered calmly. By now, the DUST OFF had taken several hits. As Kelly continued to float over the area, he was told repeatedly to leave, that the area was too hot. Hot landing zones were nothing new to Kelly. Lately, they were the only kind he had encountered. Now, he was determined to get the patients on the ground and get the hell out. As Kelly started to settle into the landing zone, the helicopter suddenly pitched up, nosed over to the right and beat itself to death on the ground. "My God," Kelly gasped. A bullet had come through the open cargo door, the door the medic and crew chief were prepared to load the wounded through, barely missing the back of his seat, and struck Major Kelly in the heart. Instinctively, he pulled up on the collective and, as he slumped forward, he pushed the cyclic control. It had all happened too fast and too close to the ground for Anderson to take control of the aircraft. In an instant it had happened. The worst nightmare the 57th could possibly imagine had suddenly come true. Major Charles L. Kelly was dead, the 149th American to die in Vietnam, and the first DUST OFF pilot.

The rest of the crew, badly shaken but not seriously injured, crawled out of the mangled Huey and dragged Kelly behind a mound of dirt. The doctor broke his leg during the crash and Anderson received abrasions and contusions. Another helicopter evacuated the crew, Kelly, and the doctor to Long Vinh, but the Vietnamese still had casualties in the field. Captain Pat Brady and Lieutenant Ernest Sylvester, devastated by the news that Kelly was dead, climbed into their DUST OFF, determined to complete Kelly's mission. They flew out to the area, which was bordered on one side by a river, skirted with a dense growth of trees. One side of the landing zone Kelly had tried so hard to make was bounded by a small stream running off the Mekong River. There, lying on its side by the small stream, was Kelly's broken Huey. Brady and Sylvester wanted to complete the mission as soon as possible. With no regard for tactical flying, they shot an approach directly into the landing zone. The Viet Cong promptly opened fire, hitting the aircraft several times. They immediately retreated behind the stand of trees and worked out a different approach. This time they lost their altitude well short of the landing zone, low-leveled across the small stream and set down quickly. They had given the VC very little chance to fire on them and they completed Kelly's last mission safely.

That night, Captain Brady slept in Kelly's bed at Soc Trang. It was the 1st of July and Kelly had promised him that he could take over the 57th's operations in the Delta on this date, no matter what. Kelly kept that promise.

The next day, Brady had a meeting with the 13th Aviation Battalion Commander, the senior Aviation Advisor in the Delta. After expressing his sorrow on the loss of Kelly, the lieutenant colonel asked Brady if the 57th would make any operational changes, would they exercise more caution, take fewer risks? Brady's answer was "no" on all counts. It would be business as usual, Brady told him. They would continue to fly the only way they knew—the way Kelly had taught them. This was not the answer the colonel was looking for, but it was the answer he got. While not completely satisfied with Brady's view of DUST OFF's mission, in the end the colonel had no choice but to accept it. With those issues settled, there was very little left to talk about. As Brady started to leave, the commander called him back.

"I think you should have this, Captain," the colonel told Brady, handing him a small brown envelope.

"What is it, sir?" Brady asked as he accepted the envelope.

"It's the bullet that killed your boss.' Brady thanked him, stuck the envelope in his pocket, and walked out.

The news of Kelly's death quickly swept through the country, reaching into every tiny base camp and outpost. The effect was astounding. He was awarded the Distinguished Service Cross posthumously by the United States. The South Vietnamese government bestowed the Military Order Medal of Vietnam, Fifth Class, and the Cross of Gallantry with Palm. Senior Vietnamese officials sent their condolences, along with senior American officials. General William Westmoreland, who had recently been placed in command of all American military forces in South Vietnam, expressed his sorrow. General Stilwell wept when he heard of Kelly's death.

With such an outpouring of praise and honors for this man of mercy, things would never be the same for medical evacuation in the war zone. With his life, Kelly had made the final payment on the insurance policy that would guarantee the continued existence of DUST

A slightly bashful-looking Maj. Charles Kelly (right) presents a plaque to Brig. Gen. Joseph W. Silwell in June 1964, shortly before Stilwell's departure from Vietnam. The five red crosses on the plaque represented the five DUST OFF aircraft that Stilwell had grounded when the 57th first went to Vietnam. The incident still rankled. Kelly told Stilwell, "Here, General. You wanted my goddamned aircraft. Take them." Four days later Kelly was killed.

OFF. His death resolved, once and for all, the issue of portable red crosses. Suddenly, all branches of the Surgeon General's office were solidly behind the DUST OFF concept. Plans were quickly drawn up to get another helicopter ambulance detachment in country as soon as possible. The irony was impossible to escape. The political battles that Kelly had engaged in while living were easily won, now that he was gone. Quite literally, Kelly had died for DUST OFF. As the war grew in intensity, no one would ever again question the wisdom of dedicating helicopters for the sole mission of evacuating wounded. DUST OFF had finally arrived, the hard way, but it had arrived to stay.

Each new pilot entering the DUST OFF business would learn of Kelly and the standards he had set. They were expected, in no uncertain terms, to maintain those standards, regardless of rules, regulations and restrictions placed on medical evacuation. They were to fly as if Kelly was sitting in the right seat on every mission. The tradition and mystique would deepen over the years as the reputation of DUST OFF grew. There would be other pilots and crew members that would make extraordinary contributions to the legacy, but there could be only one Kelly. And many others would die in the jungles and rice paddies and mountains. They, too, would add to the rich tapestry of the legacy. However, Kelly had brought the right attitude to the high risk business of flying evacuation missions when it was needed the most. He was putting his ass on the block every day when DUST OFF's critics were most vocal. Kelly set the standards. No compromise. No rationalization. No hesitation. Fly the mission. Now. And so, he became the embodiment of the perfect DUST OFF pilot, the one you would want to come and get you if your guts were hanging, at night, in the rain, surrounded by Viet Cong. This was the legacy that Kelly left and this was his most priceless contribution.

Fortunately, the 57th had no shortage of qualified officers to take over after Kelly's death. Captain Paul Bloomquist, now the senior officer, officially assumed command of the 57th on the 2nd of July. This wasn't much of a change since he had been running things in Saigon while Kelly was in the Delta with Detachment A. Captain Brady was in charge at Soc Trang, reporting to Bloomquist. Under this arrangement, the 57th was ready to carry on with the Kelly tradition.

By August 1964, US troop strength in Vietnam had reached 18,000. However, there were events taking place in August that would soon send troop levels through the roof. On August 2nd, the US Navy destroyer Maddox was attacked by North Vietnamese torpedo boats in the Gulf of Tonkin off the coast of Vietnam in international waters. The Maddox returned fire and called in fighter planes from the aircraft carrier Ticonderoga. The US Navy sank two of the three attacking boats and damaged the other. Two days later, the communist boats attacked the Maddox again and its sister destroyer, the Turner Joy. In response to the second attack, President Johnson ordered a retaliatory attack by Navy fighter-bombers on the North Vietnamese oil tanks and torpedo boat bases at Vinh. On August 7th, the US congress overwhelmingly passed the Southeast Asia Resolution, which became commonly known as the Tonkin Gulf Resolution. This important piece of legislation gave the president full congressional authority to take all necessary measures to repel any armed attack against the forces of the United States and to prevent further aggression.

The war in Vietnam had just passed an important milestone. With the adoption of the Tonkin Gulf Resolution and the vague wording it contained, it was simply a matter of time before the American involvement in Vietnam would grow beyond the advisory effort and begin the transition into a much more direct military role. The stage was now set for a massive build-up of US forces.

August also brought the realization to the Army leadership that one detachment of five helicopters was woefully inadequate to cover all of South Vietnam. Kelly had been saying this for months, but it took his death to finally shake up the command structure. The Surgeon General's office was ordered to identify five more detachments that could be sent to the combat zone.

The order wasn't really necessary. The Surgeon General was already working on getting more DUST OFFs into the combat zone. On 15 October, the first of these additional units arrived in Vietnam. This new unit, the 82d Medical Detachment, Helicopter Ambulance, spent their first night in Vietnam doubled up with their counterparts in the 57th at Tan Son Nhut Airbase. The veterans of the 57th gave the new guys in the 82d a heavy dose of war stories that night. The next morning, the men of the 82d thanked their hosts and departed for their new home at Soc Trang. Their first sight of home, the small air strip with the tiny village at one end, just lying there in the middle of rice paddies, with only three rolls of concertina wire around the edge of it all, was not very impressive.

On the 26th of October, the 82d's Hueys arrived in the port city of Vung Tau on the South China Sea. After the maintenance team checked them out, the pilots of the 82d flew their brand new UH-1Bs to their home at Soc Trang.

In order to insure that the 82d got off to a good start, three of the most experienced pilots from the 57th were transferred to the 82d. The 57th, in turn, took three green pilots from the 82d to train. This maneuver also insured that the Kelly tradition would take root in the new unit.

The 82d's commander, Major Henry Capozzi, was a good deal more conservative in his approach to flying DUST OFF than Kelly had been. He counseled his pilots to refuse missions if there was no direct radio contact with the ground forces, and that night missions should be flown only in extreme emergencies. Capozzi had little success, however, in making his pilots cautious. Despite his orders, the veterans at Soc Trang quietly instructed the new pilots in the proper protocol of flying DUST OFF missions. The Kelly spirit was alive and well and was taking root in the 82nd.

As the 82d started settling into Soc Trang, they soon discovered that they needed a radio call sign. Several were considered and tested, including Windmill, which had been the call sign of the 49th Medical Detachment in Korea. However, it didn't seem to make much difference what the 82d called itself—the units on the ground insisted on calling them DUST OFF. If any unit flew medical evacuation missions and had red crosses on their helicopters, then that unit was DUST OFF as far as the men on the ground were concerned.

No one had anticipated or even considered this to be a problem since the 57th had successfully fought to retain the DUST OFF call sign. Now, with another medical detachment in country, this was starting to be a very real operational problem aside from being embarrassing to the 82d. When the 82d would respond to a mission and identify themselves with a call sign other than DUST OFF, the unit on the ground was confused; in one instance, the advisor on the ground notified the 82d that they would wait for the real DUST OFF. This somewhat awkward situation was relieved when the new commander of the 57th, Major Howard Huntsman, allowed the 82d to use DUST OFF. To some of the older pilots in the 57th, this rang of heresy, but there really was no other choice. In the final analysis, both units performed the same mission and a common call sign, particularly one that had as much emotional attachment as DUST OFF, would eliminate any confusion for the troops on the ground.

One Kelly tradition did die, however, when the 82d assumed the major responsibility for medical evacuation in the Delta. No longer would DUST OFF pilots be required to fly the nightly circuit. Capozzi felt that shopping for business was a waste of time, aside from being extremely dangerous.

In any event, the 57th's Detachment A was now relieved of duty at Soc Trang, so they went to Saigon and rejoined the rest of the unit. In early November, for the first time in almost two years, the 57th was together again at Tan Son Nhut in Saigon. Now, the Delta

Not all DUST OFFs had door gunners even though enemy activity around landing zones often required crew members to provide covering fire while the wounded were loaded. Here a crew chief stands guard while the medic goes after the wounded.

Just after the 82nd Medical Detachment became operational in the fall of 1964, this helicopter was hit by VC groundfire near Bac Lieu in the Delta. One bullet went through the red cross and struck a wounded Vietnamese soldier in the head, killing him instantly. Two of the surviving crew, 1st Lt. Armand Simmons and Capt. Charles Clark point to the hole made by the well-aimed bullet.

could be covered with the five DUST OFFs of the 82d, and III Corps could be covered by the reunited 57th. This buildup in medical evacuation did not come too soon.

As 1964 drew to a close, the enemy stepped up the pace of the war. On 1 November, Bien Hoa Air Base, approximately 20 miles northeast of Saigon, came under a heavy mortar attack. Shrapnel from the exploding mortar rounds ripped gaping holes in above-ground fuel bladders. When the flowing fuel caught fire, it engulfed several aircraft.

Bombs onboard the aircraft exploded, and the destruction quickly spread up and down the flight line. Four Americans were killed and 72 wounded. Five B-57 Canberra bombers were destroyed and 15 other aircraft damaged. Before it was all over, the 57th committed four of its five DUST OFFs to Bien Hoa.

This attack on Bien Hoa gave the Viet Cong confidence and they began conducting other, large-scale, multi-battalion assaults. They successfully employed this new tactic on 9-10 December in both Binh Dinh and Quang Tin Provinces. The losses to the Vietnamese military and civilian population quickly increased.

This new trend toward large unit operations did not cause the Viet Cong to give up terrorists attacks. These were also on the increase. On Christmas Eve, an enemy agent drove a small car beneath the porticoed half of the Brinks Hotel on Hai Ba Troung Street in downtown Saigon, parked it, and walked away. A moment later, two hundred and fifty pounds of plastic explosives ripped the hotel apart, killing 2 Americans and wounding 58. Intelligence reports later confirmed that the intended target of this attack was the Bob Hope USO troupe, which had been scheduled to spend the night in the hotel. Fortunately, they weren't there.

In the Delta, enemy activity was also on the increase. In late December, two Viet Cong regiments, the 271st and the 272d, joined forces and formed the 9th Viet Cong Division. They were equipped with the Chinese version of the Soviet AK-47 fully automatic assault rifle. The suspicion that the enemy had the AK-47 had been confirmed earlier in December when South Vietnamese forces captured a number of them during a battle in Ba Xuyen Province. With this weapon, the enemy greatly increased his firepower and increased, as well, the threat to the DUST OFFs.

On the 28th of December, the newly created 9th Division decided to demonstrate the effectiveness of their new weapons in a battle for Binh Gia, a small Catholic village on Route 2, forty miles southeast of Saigon. For three days, the enemy attacked and virtually destroyed the South Vietnamese 33d Ranger and 4th Marine Battalions. They also inflicted heavy losses on the forces that came to the aid of these beleaguered units. During this battle, the VC did not hit and run—they stood and fought a pitched battle.

The South Vietnamese losses were staggering. They suffered over 400 casualties and lost more than 200 weapons. The 82d, still getting acquainted to the demanding world of high risk evacuation missions, simply could not handle the DUST OFF requirements and called on the veterans of the 57th to assist. Together, the two DUST OFF units rescued hundreds of South Vietnamese. Nine American crewmen from downed helicopters supporting the operation were also flown from the battlefield. December was a brutal month for the South Vietnamese military. They suffered 987 killed, 2,071 wounded and 994 missing in action. The South Vietnamese civilian population suffered horrible losses, also. The VC slaughtered hundreds of civilians, including children, old people and women, suspected of supporting the government. These vicious killings were designed to show the people what happened if they opposed the Viet Cong. Finally, the true face of the enemy was emerging in the hamlets and rice paddies of South Vietnam, and it was the face of terror.

As a result of the scale and intensity of the enemy's attack at Binh Gia, President Johnson was urged by his key advisers to retaliate by bombing North Vietnam. General Westmoreland, MACV Commander, also demanded that North Vietnam be hit and hit hard. Johnson, however, hampered by indecision and uncertain how the American public would react, hesitated to take any decisive action. Incredibly, Johnson, who had fought so hard for the authority he was granted by way of the Tonkin Gulf Resolution in August, was reluctant to exercise this new power in the face of the enemy's increasing escalation of violence. In fact, it wasn't until 7 February, 1965, when the Viet Cong attacked an American base in Pleiku, killing 8 Americans and wounding 109, that Johnson was forced to take action or lose all credibility. Within hours of this attack, 49 US Navy jets destroyed North Vietnamese Army barracks and other military targets north of the Demilitarized Zone. Two days later, Johnson agreed to a policy of "sustained reprisal" against the North. This air attack represented the first overt application of the Rostow Doctrine, named after its author, Walt Rostow, a hawkish State Department official, which stated that pressure needed to be exerted against those that initiated aggression, in order to make them pay a heavy price for their actions.

The year 1964 had brought dramatic changes to the pace and tempo of the war. At years end, 23,000 Americans were in the combat zone, and America's involvement was growing rapidly. The North Vietnamese and Viet Cong had decided to widen the war and the South Vietnamese, along with their American allies, were trying desperately to keep up.

It was becoming apparent that, if South Vietnam was going to survive, American main force combat units would have to be committed to the war. To make matters even worse, the South Vietnamese government's problems were not confined to the battlefield. Since Diem's death in 1963, no fewer than eight regimes had been formed in Saigon. None proved equal to the task of governing the country. Most of this confusion would end on 11 June 1965, when Nguyen Van Thieu formed the National Leadership Committee.

However, as 1964 mercifully ended, storm clouds were forming over Vietnam. The young DUST OFF pilots could sense a new surge and sense of urgency in America's war effort. The early years, from 1962 through 1964, had been a time to learn. Now, they would be called on to show what they had learned, and apply it on a massive scale in the same tradition of courage and unhesitating service that they had forged in the early years. "When I have your wounded" would become much more than Chuck Kelly's last words—it would become a motto and would grow into an obsession.

Here, a combat medic provides treatment to a wounded soldier while waiting for DUST OFF. The combat medics were a key link in the treatment chain for the wounded. Their job was to keep the wounded alive until DUST OFF got there.

5

The System Grows Up
(1965: MEDEVAC Arrives)

The new year offered no relief from Viet Cong attacks. On 10 February 1965, VC saboteurs struck again. This time their target was a four-story hotel that housed enlisted men in Qui Nhon. The explosion killed 23 Americans and wounded 21.

General Westmoreland had had enough. On 22 February, he formally and forcefully demanded combat troops to defend military installations. On 8 March the first of these units, a battalion landing team of the 9th Marine Expeditionary Brigade, landed at Da Nang.

While these incoming units would provide security for installations, they had little effect on terrorist bombings. On 30 March, a powerful bomb exploded outside the hotel that served as the US Embassy near the Saigon River. This time the death toll was 21, including 2 Americans, and the number of wounded exceeded 200.

While the Viet Cong were capturing headlines, the DUST OFF business was growing. As Washington and Saigon wrestled with the issues involved in developing some kind of coherent strategy to counter the growing communist threat, the DUST OFF pilots kept right on flying evacuation missions and saving lives. Enthusiasm for flying, coupled with the freedom of single ship missions gave birth to a DUST OFF tradition called "scarfing."

It soon became a way of life for many of the pilots. Scarfing meant that the DUST OFF pilots would aggressively compete with each other for the wounded. It involved hunting for missions where ever possible, taking other DUST OFF's missions if you heard the request over the radio and could get there first, or attempting to beat the other DUST OFF to a pick up if two or more aircraft were in the air at the same time. In the 57th, Major Paul Bloomquist had nearly perfected the art of "scarfing missions," with Captain Doug Moore and Lieutenants Mike Trader and Jim Truscott competing with each other in hours flown and patients evacuated.

By their very nature, DUST OFF pilots were a very competitive breed; it was only natural that, eventually, they would compete with each other. In many ways, scarfing was simply a new version of Kelly's patient hunting the year before. Obviously, scarfing was not an officially sanctioned practice. Neither the commander of the 57th nor the 82d approved of the practice, but it continued none the less. By making a game of the deadly business of flying combat evacuations, the DUST OFF pilots gave a human dimension to a profession that often bordered on the insane. It was all part of the prestige, mystique, and honor of being a DUST OFF pilot. The ghost of Chuck Kelly was still riding in the right seat and the good pilots never forgot that. The advisors on the ground were aware of scarfing and they greatly approved of it, often helping the pilots keep score. They had direct radio contact with DUST OFFs practically every day and frequently were able to get their wounded to a hospital long before the request would have passed through channels.

Not all missions involved evacuating soldiers. Often, if the situation warranted, civilians were flown to medical facilities. On March 25th, the 57th flew a mission deep into the tangled mangrove swamps southeast of Saigon known as the Rung Sat Special Zone. An American advisor had called, requesting an urgent DUST OFF for a very pregnant Vietnamese woman. The advisor reported she was bleeding profusely and he feared she was miscarrying. Major Huntsman, along with Captain Doug Moore, co-pilot, and Staff Sergeant Charles Allen, medic, accepted the mission. The Rung Sat Special Zone was one of the Viet Cong's major areas of operations, which meant this DUST OFF was extremely likely to take ground fire. After landing at the tiny hamlet of Phuoc Khanh, Allen loaded the woman aboard, made her as comfortable as possible and they took off. As expected, the VC fired a few rounds at the Huey, but scored no hits. As they raced to Saigon, Mother Nature took over and Allen performed the first mid-air delivery in Vietnam—a wailing, healthy 5 pound baby boy. Allen wrapped the infant in his fatigue shirt and presented him to his mother as the DUST OFF landed at Cong Hoa Hospital.

April the 1st was not a good day for DUST OFF. On that day, a Vietnamese Ranger Battalion had engaged a large, dug-in VC force near the village of Duc Hoa, 15 miles west of Saigon. The intense fighting had produced several casualties. Specialist Wayne C. Simmons was the medic on board the first DUST OFF from the 57th to arrive on the scene. As the DUST OFF approached the landing zone, four Vietnamese carried a wounded American sergeant toward the helicopter. Suddenly, the VC opened up on the landing zone with .30 caliber machine gun fire and mortars. The barrage killed the American and two of the Vietnamese. Simmons leaped from the helicopter and began loading wounded as the enemy fire intensified. He had loaded seven

This shot captures all the elements of an evacuation that the DUST OFF crews always hoped for—a secure landing zone, communication with the unit on the gound, and medics treating the wounded. Naturally, they rarely got it this way.

patients before the heavy fire forced DUST OFF out of the area, leaving Simmons on the ground. A second DUST OFF, piloted by Doug Moore, made repeated attempts to get in and pick up Simmons, but the mortar and machine gun fire made it impossible. Darkness came with Simmons still out there on the ground.

The next morning, Paul Bloomquist flew over the area looking for Simmons. They found the dead sergeant first. Nearby they found Simmons, also dead, with wounds in the head and shoulder.

Specialist 5 Wayne Simmons died the most highly decorated enlisted man in the war at that time. He had flown over 200 combat missions. Simmons was also the first enlisted man to die flying DUST OFFs, but he would not be the last.

On May 3d, the 173d Airborne Brigade joined the Marines, becoming the first US Army combat unit committed to South Vietnam. The arrival of the 173d coincided with renewed larger-scale enemy attacks.

During May, a VC regimental force attacked the capital of Phuoc Long Province in the west of III Corps, and then ambushed and destroyed a South Vietnamese battalion sent to relieve the Province capital. In June, the enemy again dealt the ARVN a staggering blow in the battle of Don Xoai, 55 miles northeast of Saigon.

As the war picked up momentum, the DUST OFF units, like all other US units in Vietnam, were plagued with an influx of reporters from the US eager to file a story—any story—involving American forces. The press corps had greatly increased in size since Temperelli dealt with reporters in Nha Trang back in the summer of 1962, yet one thing had remained the same; the reporters still wanted dramatic, gripping stories. Some newsmen made pests of themselves and, when this happened, the DUST OFF crews would occasionally have a little fun at the reporters expense. Since most of the reporters in Vietnam had no military experience, it was relatively easy to tell them just about anything and have it published in a national media outlet.

One day in late June, a particularly bothersome reporter showed up at the 57ths headquarters at Tan Son Nhut. He explained that he was from TIME magazine and that he was going to write a story about the All American Boy—a DUST OFF pilot who daily and routinely subjected himself to hostile fire, protected only by red crosses. Unfortunately, the reporter soon found himself talking to Captain Doug Moore and Lieutenant Jim Troscott, two of the 57th's most notorious practical jokers who never passed up an opportunity to have a little fun. They pretended to be very impressed that a reporter from TIME would want to interview them.

"The guy you really want to talk to is Major Bloomquist", Troscott told the reporter. "He's the greatest DUST OFF pilot we've got."

"You mean he's better than you guys?" the reporter asked, growing excited.

"Much better," Troscott deadpanned. "We're good. But Bloomquist is the best."

"Where is he?" the reporter demanded eagerly.

"Where he always is. Out flying missions. The man never stops," Moore added. Troscott nodded solemnly in agreement.

They spoke glowingly of Bloomquists love of the war, his courage and how he stayed awake at night, thinking of new and better ways to improve DUST OFF. They even created a nickname for Bloomquist on the spot—Big Bear, and they decided to give him more decorations and citations than he had earned. As Bloomquist's exploits grew, the reporter couldn't get enough. When he asked for more details, Moore and Troscott gave them to him. Ed Taylor, another pilot, intruded on this deception, quickly grasped what was going on, and added to it. After about an hour, the reporter was convinced that Big Bear Bloomquist was the greatest, bravest pilot who had ever flown. When Bloomquist finally returned, the reporter clung to him like a leech, demanding even more detailed exploits from the man himself. Unaware of what his buddies had done to the reporter, Bloomquist finally told him to get the hell out. After he left, Bloomquist demanded to know what was going on. Moore and Truscott promptly confessed, and they all had a good laugh and wondered if a story would actually be written that would detail Big Bear Bloomquist's exploits.

They didn't have to wait long. The July 2d issue of TIME carried a very long, prominent story entitled, *The Gamest Bastards of All,* yet clearly the emphasis was on "Big Bear Bloomquist." The article was a very accurate reflection of what Moore and Truscott gave the reporter. At that point, any relation to facts and the article ceased to exist. "Through the end of last year," the article stated, "fully 20% of the personnel in Bloomquists detachment had been killed in action and another 45% wounded, even though their unarmed, unarmored

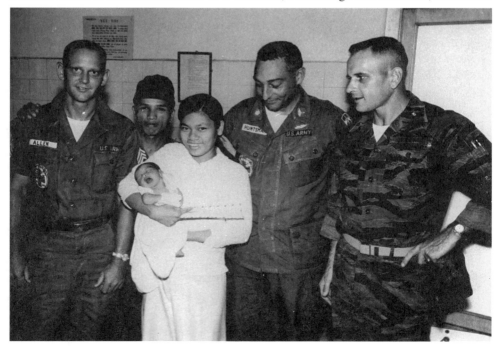

This little guy with his proud Vietnamese parents was the first "airborne" delivery by a DUST OFF. On 25 March, 1965, SSG Charles Allen (left) delivered the 5-pound baby boy en route to Saigon in a helicopter piloted by Maj. Huntsman (cetner). The delivery was yet another Vietnam first for the pioneering 57th.

A DUST OFF brings wounded soldiers of the 101st Air Cavalry Division to the fire base Berchtesgaden for treatment.

ships are clearly marked with red crosses on their noses." While not true, the statement does have dramatic impact. However, the part that caused the most laughter in the 57th came near the end of the article as the reporter attempted to describe a typical mission. "Bloomquist found himself swooping in behind four fighter-bombers to pick up seven wounded Americans. Suddenly, one of the escorting Skyraiders burst into flames from a ground hit, and its partners peeled away to protect it. All alone, Bloomquist's chopper—call sign 'Dust-off 174'—touched down amid withering crossfire from Viet Cong .50-cal. Machine guns. Bloomquist ordered his crew to load the wounded, calmly polished his sunglasses, then rotated out in a hail of tracers."

For weeks after the article, Bloomquist was known both as "Big Bear" and "John Wayne." He took the ribbing with a good sense of humor, even when some of the other pilots offered to polish his sunglasses. Such diversions were not only fun, but necessary, for they allowed the DUST OFF crews to escape, ever so briefly, the harsh realities of war.

In July, the fighting shifted to the Central Highlands, the rugged, mountainous area to the north and northwest of Saigon. A series of South Vietnamese defeats in this area caused serious concern that the enemy might actually succeed in cutting the country in half, roughly on a line from Pleiku to the coast at Qui Nhon.

At least four North Vietnamese divisions were operating in the South at this time, supporting the Viet Cong. These divisions represented tens of thousands of North Vietnamese regular forces, making a mockery of communists claims that the war in the South was nothing more than the "people's revolution." This large number of North Vietnamese forces was nothing short of a massive invasion of the Republic of South Vietnam. It was becoming increasingly clear that the US build-up would have to be quick and that the enemy offensive would have to be blunted if the Saigon government was to survive.

General Westmoreland and his staff made a strong, forceful case for additional manpower. Without it, the general explained to Washington, democracy in the South would soon cease to exist and the communist tide would consume all of Southeast Asia. In August, the 1st Cavalry Division (Air Mobile), better known as the 1st Cav, arrived in country and deployed to the Central Highlands. With headquarters in An Khe, 35 miles inland from Qui Nhon, the 1st Cav brought a new dimension to the war. Over 450 helicopters of various types would allow this division to move combat forces rapidly, over a large area. For the first time, the US Army had a whole division, roughly 16,000 soldiers, capable of being moved by helicopter. The arrival of the 1st Cav marked the beginning of the real build-up of American combat forces in South Vietnam. It also marked the beginning of a dramatic shift in the way the war was going to be fought. No longer would US forces simply assume a role of advising the South Vietnamese military. US forces would now engage in direct combat with the enemy. From this point forward, Vietnam would, in all aspects, be America's war.

The rugged terrain of the Central Highlands would not prevent the 1st Cav from conducting large scale operations throughout the entire region. Combat operations would be limited only by the range of the helicopters. Reinforcements could now be moved quickly to where they were needed most.

The 1st Cav also had its own medical evacuation unit, making it the first and only US Army combat unit to have its own evacuation helicopters. The Air Ambulance Platoon, which consisted of 12 helicopters and crews, was an integral part of the division's 15th Medical Battalion. This platoon was equipped with the third generation of Hueys—the brand new UH-1D. This new version had a longer body, longer rotor blades for greater lift, and a more powerful turbine engine.

While the Air Ambulance Platoon was modeled on the concept of the medical detachments such as the 57th and 82d, the pilots of the Air Ambulance Platoon used the call sign MEDEVAC which was readily understood to mean medical evacuation. The platoon also started the practice of allowing Warrant Officers to fly medical evacuation missions in Vietnam.

The Air Ambulance Platoon went to work almost immediately, and quickly learned the value of good communications. On 19 September, four of the platoon's helicopters flew in support of one of the 1st Cavs first combat operations. The landing zone was under heavy fire and, due to poor coordination, confusion and the stress of combat, the wounded soldiers were loaded on the troop carrying helicopters and the dead were placed on the MEDEVAC helicopters. This tragic error probably cost two of the soldiers their lives since there was no one medically trained on the troop carrying helicopters to treat them. Incidents such as this clearly illustrated the unguent need for dedicated medical evacuation helicopters.

On October 10th, the Air Ambulance Platoon lost its first helicopter supporting an operation near Qui Nhon. While patients were loaded on board Captain Guy Kimsey's MEDEVAC, several Viet Cong rounds slammed into the engine and immediately shut down the aircraft. Another MEDEVAC was quickly summoned and when it arrived, Kimsey, his crew and the patients were flown out. However, before the downed helicopter could be recovered, an artillery round scored a direct hit on the disabled bird, completely destroying it.

Unfortunately, the helicopter was not the only loss the platoon would suffer that day. Captain Charles F. Kane was supporting Operation Shiny Bayonet near An Khe when his ship came under fire. While hovering near the ground, Kane was struck in the head by a VC bullet. The co-pilot flew immediately to the 85th Evacuation Hospital at Qui Nhon in a desperate effort to save Kane's life, but the captain was already dead. He was the first pilot of the Air Ambulance Platoon to die in Vietnam.

During October and into November, the 1st Cav battled with four North Vietnamese regiments in an area 30 miles southwest of Pleiku known as the Ia Drang Valley, all too commonly called the Valley of Death. The number of wounded varied from day to day, but averaged 70 to 80. On the worst day, 200 men were wounded. During this major, bloody battle, the Air Ambulance Platoon more than proved its worth. Most of the evacuations were carried out under heavy enemy fire, in very rugged terrain. In many ways, the Central Highlands proved to be the most difficult terrain in South Vietnam.

Aside from the number of wounded, the rough, mountainous terrain and the constant enemy fire, the Ia Drang Campaign presented the platoon with another problem. Dense, 100 foot tall trees had prevented the evacuation of soldiers from the spot where they were wounded. The dense jungle forced the ground troops to move their wounded comrades to locations where they could be picked up. One battalion commander involved in the battle wrote in his after action report: "I lost many leaders killed and wounded while recovering casualties. Wounded must be pulled back to some type of covered position and then treated. Troops must not get so concerned with the casualties that they forget the enemy and their mission. Attempting to carry a man requires up to four men as (litter) bearers, which can devastate a unit at a critical time."

Rather than attempt to restrain a soldier's natural concern for his wounded comrades, this major problem of plucking the wounded out of the jungle would eventually be solved with technical innovation—the hoist.

On 27 August, 1965, the 283d Medical Detachment, Helicopter Ambulance, arrived at Qui Nhon. The 283d was the third DUST OFF unit assigned to Vietnam. The men were glad that the 24 day ordeal aboard the aging World War II transport, the *USS Blatchford,* was over. Well into the Pacific crossing, the *Blatchford's* engine had quit. For days, the old ship drifted helplessly as the crew repaired the ancient engine. Finally, after reaching Qui Nhon, the men of the 283d thought they were free of the *Blatchford*. This, however, was not to be. At some point during the long crossing, the 283rd's destination had been changed to Saigon. With barely a chance to look around Qui Nhon, the 283rd reboarded the *Blatchford* and

His face showing a mixture of caution and concern, a DUST OFF crew chief helps to lift a wounded Viet Cong aboard a Huey at Bam Me Thuot. During the course of the war medical evacuation units rescued soldiers of all nations, including enemy NVS troops from North Vietnam.

limped slowly down the coast to Saigon, joining forces with the 57th at Tan Son Nhut. On the 15th of September, the 283d declared itself operational and went into the DUST OFF business, following in what was now becoming the grand tradition of the 57th.

By the fall of 1965, there was no longer a question of the tremendous contributions DUST OFF units had made—and would make—in support of combat operations. The time had now come to deploy a larger version of the detachment in order to cover wider operational areas and better coordinate coverage under one commander. In September, this larger DUST OFF unit—the Medical Company, Air Ambulance,—arrived in Vietnam. With headquarters in Nha Trang, where it had all started over three years earlier, the 498th Medical Company, commanded by Lieutenant Colonel Joseph P. Madrano, became operational on the 20th of September. His mission was to cover all of II Corps with his 25 UH-1D DUSTOFFs. He could choose his own bases, yet he was required to support all tactical units in the II Corps area, with the exception of the 1st Cav, which had its own Air Ambulance Platoon.

The UH-1D was, by far, the best Huey to date in the proud line being produced by Bell Helicopter. It still had the basic T53-L-11 engine with modifications, but the rotor diameter was increased to 48 feet and the width of the main rotor was increased to 21 inches. These changes nearly doubled the payload of the basic UH-1. The UH-1D could take up to 14 passengers, or could carry nearly 4,000 pounds of cargo. Its arrival, with the 498th, was

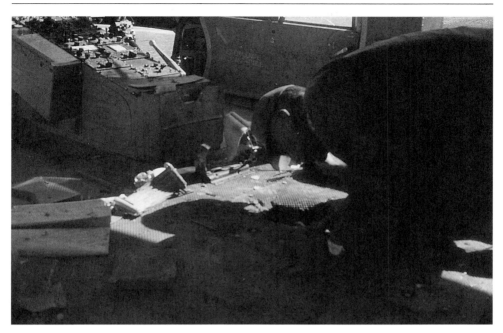

Maj. Glenn Bracken of the 498th Medical Company (Air Ambulance) examines a DUST OFF helicopter shot down by a VC near Tuy Hoea in the spring of 1966. Enemy gunners considered DUST OFFs highly prized targets and would often lay an ambush near a pick-up zone where the helicopters were at their most vulnerable and least able to take avoiding action.

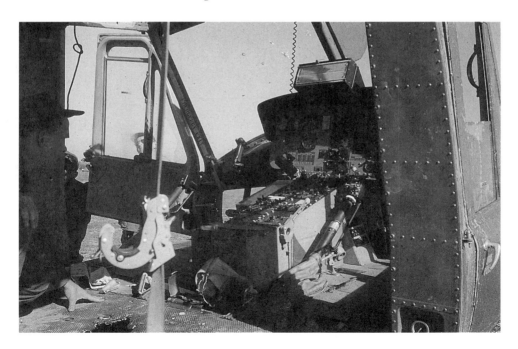

timely. Colonel Madrano divided his company into platoons in order to cover his territory. He stationed one and a half platoons at Qui Nhon to cover the coastal plains from Tuy Hoa north to the An Khe Valley in the west, one and a half platoons at Pleiku in the Central Highlands, and the remainder of the company, including maintenance, at Nha Trang to cover the southern section of II Corps.

While the dispersion was as good as Madrano could make it and it did provide excellent DUST OFF support, it also created monumental problems for the company. Maintenance had to be carried out at three separate locations. What Madrano was discovering had actually been discovered by Temperelli three and a half years earlier. The only difference now was that it was happening on a larger scale. Madrano found himself flying constantly around his far-flung command, coordinating operations and solving problems.

However, the 498th made the necessary adjustments and soon got down to the serious business of flying DUST OFFs. On November the 11th, the 3rd Platoon, which had been assigned to Qui Nhon, received a DUST OFF request from a South Korean unit operating east of An Khe. Major Burroughs, the platoon commander, and First Lieutenant Roger Hula flew the mission. Things were uneventful until the DUST OFF prepared to leave the landing zone with the wounded Korean safely on board. Suddenly, enemy soldiers began firing on the aircraft at close range. One round came through the windshield and struck Burroughs in the neck. Hula, the copilot, glanced to his left, saw blood spurting from Burroughs' neck and grabbed the controls. By now, the Viet Cong were standing in front of the helicopter, firing at point-blank range.

"Shoot the bastards!" Hula shouted into the intercom to the crew chief in the back as he pulled in all the power available and made a forward, low-level take-off. With Viet Cong directly in his path, Hula kept going as the crew chief fired his M-14 rifle out of the open cargo door. When his ammo was gone, the crew chief leaned out the door and clubbed two enemy soldiers with the butt of his rifle. Once airborne, the medic turned his attention to the wounded pilot. About the only thing the medic could do was stop the bleeding with a pressure bandage around the pilots neck, and that's what he did, with Burroughs still sitting in the left seat. Hula put the RPM indicator of his new Huey in the red zone in a desperate race to get to Qui Nhon before Burroughs or the Korean died. And he made it. Both Burroughs and the Korean recovered, thanks to the quick decisive action of the crew and the powerful, new Huey that performed when it had to.

That same night, the 498th suffered its first losses. On a urgent mission to support a unit a few miles west of Qui Nhon, a DUST OFF piloted by Captain Edward Haswell and Major Richard Scott crashed into the side of a mountain during heavy fog and immediately burst into flames. Scott managed to pull Haswell from the burning wreck, but Specialist 5th Class Gilivado Martinez and Privates First Class William Esposito and Orin Allred were killed.

The last medical evacuation crewman to die in 1965 was Warrant Officer George W. Rice, a member of the 1st Cav's Air Ambulance Platoon. Rice was flying copilot on a MEDEVAC piloted by Captain Walter Berry, Jr., on December the 18th. They had just set

The buddies of a wounded trooper carry him toward the big red cross of a waiting DUST OFF. Few things in the combat zone were as certain as DUST OFF.

Bullets that ripped through the back of the pilot's seat and the interior of the cargo compartment like this led to the introduction of an extra two inches of armor plating to the back of the seat.

the helicopter on the ground and were preparing to take casualties on board when an enemy soldier popped up from a spider hole to the left of the aircraft and opened fire. The Huey took several hits before one round came through the open cargo door and hit Rice in the head. Berry raced to the nearest hospital, but it was hopeless. Warrant Officer George Rice died within the hour.

As 1965 drew to a close, it became obvious that the decision to require two pilots in each DUST OFF was a sound one. Over and over again, DUST OFFs would survive when either the pilot or copilot became a causality. However, the mere fact that the causality rate among the crews of the evacuation helicopters could have been higher was little consolation to their comrades. The Air Ambulance Platoon Commander, Major Carl J. Bobay, wrote in December: "Within three months of operations in Vietnam, two pilots have been killed, one enlisted man wounded, and nine helicopters shot up, all due to enemy action. Believe me, we are not proud of these statistics. What the next eight months may hold in store for us is too frightening to even consider."

After the incident that killed Warrant Officer Rice, the Air Ambulance Platoon began a project to mount steel plating to extend an additional six or seven inches above the back of the pilots armored seats to offer some degree of protection to the pilots heads. The 498th was also pushing for the extra armor on the seat backs. The 498th and the Air Ambulance Platoon soon concluded that, in all probability, another quarter inch of protection would have prevented Major Burroughs neck wound; an additional two inches would have saved Warrant Officer Rice's life. Due to the nature of the evacuation business, the helicopters were required to spend time on the ground under extremely dangerous circumstances. The enemy had been quick to learn that the pilots were nothing more than sitting ducks until the patients were loaded. These were lessons that could only be learned in the harsh environment of combat. There was no way the Bell Helicopter engineers back at Fort Worth could have possibly known these things. As magnificent as the new UH-1D was, it needed to be even better if the DUST OFF pilots were to survive. The pilots desperately needed any additional protection they could get. As a result, making these life saving additions to all evacuation helicopters became an extremely high priority.

The almost daily acts of heroism of combat medics under fire contributed greatly to the success of DUST OFF. This dramatic sequence clearly illustrates the courage of a medic who disregarded enemy fire to carry out a battlefield rescue.

The year 1965 had seen a rapid buildup of US forces in Vietnam. As the year ended, 184,000 Americans were assigned there, up sharply from the end of 1964. With the large influx of American military units, other dramatic changes were altering the face of this war.

During the year, 8,896 medical evacuations were flown, carrying a total of 12,456 patients. For the first time in the war, the majority of patients were American—7,364. Unfortunately, this trend would continue through 1968.

6

Reaching Perfection
(The Hoist and Other Improvements)

With the passage of time, the DUST OFF crews became increasingly proficient in their dangerous art. By the beginning of 1966, with almost four years of experience to draw from, DUST OFF had evolved into a highly specialized method of saving lives. At the same time DUST OFF was developing the most efficient methods of evacuating casualties from the battlefield, the crews were also developing doctrine that would serve as the basis for training replacement crews back in the US. The whole DUST OFF operation was in a state of constant flux. The pilots and crews made adjustments and changes based on the situations they encountered on a daily basis. These adjustments were quickly translated into policy and the policy became doctrine. Without being consciously aware of it, the DUST OFF crews operating in South Vietnam during this time frame were on the cutting edge of the specialized art of medical evacuation. Much like the surgeons in the evacuation hospitals that were springing up throughout the country, the DUST OFF pilots were experimenting with new techniques and procedures that had only one goal—saving lives.

Some things worked better than others, but nothing failed due to a lack of

A partially obscured DUST OFF can be seen through the smoke settling into the landing zone. Smoke grenades played a vital role in the evacuation by clearly identifying the unit on the ground. The smoke also provided the pilots valuable information on wind speed and direction.

effort. In short, the DUST OFF crews were writing the book on medical evacuation as they lived it. Very little in the way of innovation was driven from the top down. Almost all innovative techniques came from the bottom up. It was the epitome of the Kelly doctrine being practiced by a whole new generation of DUST OFF pilots. The success achieved was directly related to the intangible qualities of courage, skill, discipline, imagination, leadership, and teamwork.

By now, the crew of a typical DUST OFF was well defined. It consisted of the pilot, copilot, crew chief and medic. The pilot always sat in the left seat and the copilot occupied the right seat. The crew chief and medic took up positions in the cabin on either side of the aircraft. They were all connected by the intercom in their helmets that allowed them to communicate over the deafening whine of the turbine engine. This four man crew was extremely close-knit, with each crew member having critical and well-defined responsibilities. The success of any mission depended on everyone knowing what they were supposed to do and then doing it, regardless of weather, terrain, or enemy fire. Each of the four men had absolute trust in the other three. This trust became so total that it was the only thing taken for granted.

A typical request for an evacuation could come from one of several sources. The crew could be tasked at their base or in the air. If an American or allied unit had casualties, and their radio was powerful enough, they could call DUST OFF directly. The decision to request an evacuation rested with the unit's medic and senior man present. If DUST OFF could not be contacted directly, the request was passed back to the units headquarters and then on to DUST OFF. Regardless of the method used, the request had to contain certain pieces of critical information—exact location of the landing zone; the number and condition of casualties; types of wounds; radio frequency and call signs of the unit on the ground; any special needs such as oxygen or whole blood; terrain features; enemy activity at the landing zone; and weather conditions. The first four elements were critical. With them, the mission would be flown. Without them, there was no guarantee.

Human nature being what it is, there were two elements of any request for a DUST OFF that were always open to a great deal of interpretation—the condition of the wounded and the intensity of the enemy fire. Combat units on the ground wanted to get their wounded to the hospital, and often exaggerated the condition of the patients. This was understandable. Often, landing zones were reported secure when they were not. This, too, was understandable.

In an effort to add a degree of objectivity to a decidedly subjective, highly emotional issue, a patient classification system was developed. The intent was to increase efficiency and avoid needlessly launching DUST OFFs. Patients were divided into three categories: urgent, priority, and routine. Urgent patients were simply that—those in real danger of dying if not evacuated immediately. An urgent request demanded an immediate response from any available DUST OFF. Priority patients were classified as being serious but not critical. By definition, they could withstand a four hour wait or longer, if necessary. Those in the routine category would be evacuated after the urgent and priority had been taken care of. In this classification system, pain was not supposed to be a factor in making a determination. However, in practice, any patient in great pain usually drew an urgent classification and nobody complained.

Determining the security of the landing zone was often as subjective as classifying patients. Even the unit on the ground could not always accurately assess the degree of security in the battle area. Finally, a practical rule of thumb gained wide acceptance—if the unit on the ground could stand up and help load the wounded, then the landing zone was, by definition, about as secure as it could get. The tough part, of course, was that DUST OFF had to get on the ground in order to pass this acid test. For all these reasons, it was critical that radio contact be established with the ground unit when approaching a landing zone.

As always, response time was often the difference between bringing back a patient or transporting a corpse. To shave every possible second off the response time, the DUST OFF crews practiced getting airborne as quickly as they could. The goal was to be in the air in less than three minutes after receiving a request for evacuation. Any longer period was unacceptable. Once in the air, the Aircraft Commander (AC) would tune his radio to the DUST OFF frequency and receive his assignment. This technique avoided a time consuming briefing while still on the ground. At some point along the route, the AC switched to the tactical frequency of the ground unit, told them help was on the way, and collected vital information about the wounded and the landing zone. While the AC worked the radio, the

A wounded South Vietnamese soldier is carried toward a waiting DUST OFF. One of the great frustrations facing the DUST OFF crews was the poor quality of the Vietnamese medical facilities. Wounded Vietnamese troops would be flown from the battlefield at great risk to the DUST OFF crews—often to die in a Vietnamese hospital before receiving treatment.

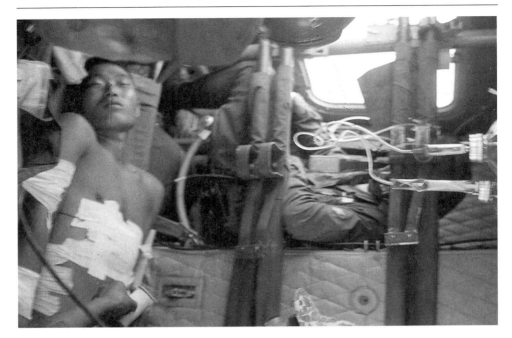

A wounded South Korean soldier lies stoically aboard a DUST OFF from the 498th Medical Detachment that is evacuating him from near Qui Nhon in 1966. The uncomplaining Korean soldiers were held in high regard by the DUST OFF crews. To solve communication problems, Korean interpreters went along to assist with the evacuation.

copilot usually flew the aircraft. In the back, the crew chief and medic made preparations for the wounded as they monitored the communications between the AC and the ground unit. Before take off, the medic had made sure that he had adequate medical supplies onboard. The crew chief, responsible for the overall flightworthiness of the aircraft, would have made sure that he had all necessary tools and equipment onboard.

At the landing zone, the crew chief and medic would quickly load the wounded, or supervise the loading by the ground unit. Often, this would be the first time the wounded had received any medical treatment. Once the patients were loaded and secured, the crew chief would tell the AC he was clear to lift off. Then the medic and crew chief would go to work treating patients.

As soon as possible after departing the landing zone, the medic would report each patients condition to the AC who, in turn, would radio this information to the nearest Medical Regulating Officer (MRO). Based on this report, the MRO would direct DUST OFF to the nearest medical facility capable of treating the most seriously wounded. Thus, the medic's initial evaluation was critical. His central focus was isolating the most seriously wounded and keeping that man alive until they reached the hospital. Where DUST OFF flew after leaving the landing zone was always dictated by the medical condition of the most seriously wounded onboard, and that assessment was made by the medic. This system worked extremely well, particularly during times of mass casualties.

The secret was teamwork. All the good crews had one thing in common—they worked smoothly and efficiently, like four well-oiled parts of a complex machine. The helicopter became an extension of the crews and, in the hands of a skilled pilot, seemed to come alive. They all knew that, in the end, whether they lived or died depended more on the helicopter than anything else. It could save them or kill them, depending on an endless number of variables, most beyond the control of the crew.

As time passed, DUST OFFs became more sophisticated and better organized, but they never got very far from the basic principles laid down by Charlie Kelly. No compromise. No rationalization. Fly the mission. Now.

Early in 1966, the fourth DUST OFF detachment arrived in country. On February the 1st, the 254th Medical Detachment declared itself operational at Long Binh, adjacent to the 93rd Evacuation Hospital, approximately 20 miles northeast of Saigon. The primary mission of the 254th was to support the 173d Airborne Brigade's sweep operations.

As more American ground forces entered the war, US combat units began pushing deeper and deeper into South Vietnam's dense jungles, relentlessly pursuing the enemy. Thus, the problem of rescuing soldiers from densely forested areas was becoming more pronounced every day. In fact, as 1966 wore on, this was considered the most critical problem that needed to be solved regarding medical evacuation.

A medic treats a wounded man at a collection point while waiting for DUST OFF. In the early years, before the advent of the jungle penetrator device, Vietnam's rugged terrain and triple-canopy jungle made many areas inaccessible to DUST OFFs, and the wounded had to be taken to collection points.

The Army considered several solutions to this problem; some quite novel, others simply silly. One of the most intriguing, which was actually tested at Fort Bragg, required the troops on the ground to strap a large, collapsible box to the upper branches of a large tree. This box would be dropped to the troops on the ground by the helicopter attempting to rescue the wounded. After strapping the box to the tree, the idea was to somehow haul the wounded up to the box, and wait while the helicopter moved into a hover directly above the box. Then, the crew chief would extend a 4-foot ladder down to the box and the wounded would be taken aboard. The absurdity of this approach was soon apparent. Wounded soldiers could not be easily moved to the top of a tree in a combat environment, and the box was difficult to secure.

Another scheme, called the "Jungle Platform System," required the helicopter crew to unroll two large stainless steel nets over the tops of dense, jungle trees. Then, if the wounded somehow miraculously managed to get to the treetops, the evacuation helicopter would hover over the nets, which could support considerable weight, and the wounded could be flown to safety. This idea, much like the box in the tree, soon died a much deserved death.

However, the problem of getting casualties out of the jungle still persisted. Since attempts to bring the patient to the helicopters weren't successful, it was now time to bring the helicopter to the patient. The solution was surprisingly simple; the introduction of the hoist.

In fact, Bell Helicopter and the Breeze Corporation of Union, New Jersey, had been working on the hoist solution for a long time. Back in 1962, the Surgeon General stated that a valid requirement existed for a light weight, reliable hoisting device for his air ambulances. The stated purpose for the hoist was "to facilitate aeromedical evacuation in support of combat forces operating in mountainous areas and over terrain or water which precludes the helicopter landing and picking up patients." The need for the hoist was immediately recognized when American units began large scale operations. In 1965, the Commanding General of the 173d Airborne Brigade send a letter to the Director of the Joint Research and Test Activity stating that there was an urgent need for a means of resupplying troops and evacuating casualties in jungle areas where sufficient clearance for landing helicopters is not available and preparation of a landing zone within the time available is unfeasible.

Now, in 1966, it appeared that the Breeze hoist was ready for a real field test. Mounted inside the top of the cargo area and anchored to the floor behind the copilots seat, the hoist could be swung outside the aircraft so that the cables and pulleys were clear of the landing skids. Powered by an electric winch, the hoist was capable of lifting 600 pounds 250 feet. Hoists proved to be extremely successful in rescuing many patients in extremely rugged terrain—patients who would otherwise have died.

A typical hoist mission required the DUST OFF to hover over the wounded and lower the cable to the ground. The first hoist systems had a specially constructed vest on the end of the cable. The wounded soldier was placed in the vest and hoisted up to the waiting medic. The idea of the hoist was as simple as it was dangerous. While it added a dramatic new capability to the DUST OFF business, there was a very serious down side to the procedure. For any hoist mission to succeed, it required the DUST OFF to remain motionless, in a high hover, above the pick-up zone while the operation was taking place. Nothing in a combat zone is quite as vulnerable as a helicopter maintaining a high hover.

The first actual hoist mission in a combat zone was flown on May 17th by Captain Donald Retzlaff, 1st Platoon, 498th Medical Company, Nha Trang, in response to an urgent request from the 1st Brigade of the 101st Airborne Division, 12 miles north of Song Be. Since the hoist was new and the ground units were unfamiliar with it, the medic rode the cable down while Retzlaff maintained a hover above the pick-up zone. Once on the ground, the medic showed the ground troops how to place the wounded in the special jacket. Tragically, the first causality to be lifted from the jungle floor was a lieutenant who had been killed only an hour earlier. However, before the day was over, 17 wounded had been hauled up using this latest innovation, demonstrating, in no uncertain terms, the tremendous potential of the hoist.

As the hoist went into general service throughout Vietnam, several improvements and refinements were made. A rigid metal litter was soon added to extract patients who were too seriously wounded to be placed in the vest. However, neither the vest nor the litter worked very well in dense jungle.

To solve this problem, the "Jungle Penetrator" was developed. The penetrator, which was attached to the end of the hoist cable, weighted 20 pounds and had three paddle-like seats that could be folded up against the sides of the penetrator's 3-foot-long, bullet-shaped body. The compact shape of the penetrator allowed it to easily drop through the jungle

As DUST OFFs became increasingly susceptible to enemy gunfire, it became necessary to beef-up the Huey's protective systems. In addition to improving the seats, a sliding armor panel was also added that could be extended to provide the pilot with limited protection from ground fire.

canopy to the troops below. Once on the ground, the seats of the penetrator were pulled down and the wounded was strapped on with chest belts. The first penetrators arrived in Vietnam in mid-June and, after extensive testing, were placed in general use by October.

As the American build up continued, DUST OFF operations became even more critical and the use of the hoist increased dramatically. However, the use of the hoist required incredible skill and courage on the part of the DUST OFF crew. During a typical hoist operation, the pilot would be simultaneously communicating with the ground unit and the medic and crew chief in the cargo bay of the helicopter. These communications were critical because the ground unit could tell the pilot where the enemy were; the crew chief could tell the pilot if he was about to make contact with a tree. It was absolutely critical that the helicopter remain motionless during the entire operation. The slightest movement 200 feet in the air is greatly magnified on the ground. During many hoist operations, the crew on board the DUST OFF could not even see the ground. As a result, the pilot had no visual reference to use as a cue to compensate for drift. This condition added enormously to the stress of holding the aircraft motionless while the men on the ground strapped the patient to the hoist.

In addition to the mental strain of monitoring the radios and the intercom while hovering motionless, not to mention the anxiety of waiting for the VC to open fire, the pilots also found the operation physically demanding. Add a strong crosswind and darkness, and the

Wounded, but how serious? The question was never easy to answer. Whether or not to call DUST OFF was a judgement call for the unit on the ground. While only the most seriously injured qualified for air evacuation, ground units often exaggerated the seriousness of a patient's condition in order to get the wounded to a hospital. Rarely would DUST OFF question the ground unit. They simply flew the mission.

Under stress—the strain of combat is clearly visible on the faces of these soldiers as they help a wounded comrade to a landing zone. After major actions there were seldom enough stretchers to go round.

degree of difficulty required for a successful hoist operation increased enormously. Yet most, if not all, of these conditions were present at the site of every hoist operation. These dangers never prevented DUST OFF from making at effort.

It didn't take the enemy long to exploit the risks of hoist missions. The first DUST OFF shot down performing a hoist mission belonged to the 283d Medical Detachment at Tan Son Nhut. On the 1st of November, Captain James Lombard and Lieutenant Melvin Ruiz were on standby when a call was received from a unit with casualties ten miles north of Saigon. Once airborne, Lombard contacted the ground unit and asked if the area was secure. The answer he received was less than reassuring. The ground unit told him there were enemy snipers in the area; however the ground unit believed they had been taken out. Lombard then called Bien Hoa to determine if gunships had been dispatched to the area to fly protective cover for his mission. Gun ship coverage for medical evacuations in a contested area had recently become policy throughout Vietnam. Lombard was told it would take thirty minutes to have gun ships over the area and he was not about to wait that long. He decided to perform the evacuation without the protective coverage. Within minutes, Lombard was over the area, prepared to make a hoist extraction of two critically wounded soldiers.

Unable to see through the dense jungle foliage, Lombard asked the ground unit to mark their location with smoke. When wisps of blue smoke drifted up through the trees, Lombard hovered over the spot while the crew chief lowered the jungle penetrator. The penetrator was only ten feet below the skids when it happened. Suddenly, the Viet Cong opened fire from the right side. Apparently, the enemy had been waiting for the arrival of DUST OFF. Immediately, the aircraft took several hits along its entire length. A second

This was the first DUST OFF equipped with the electric hoist, which was mounted just behind the copilot's seat.

Captain Don Retzlaff. He flew the first hoist mission May 1, 1966.

later, all the warning lights on the instrument panel lit up, the hydraulics were gone, and the crew could hear the loud, sickening sound of crunching and growling metal coming from the transmission.

Realizing that his Huey was fatally wounded, Lombard immediately broke off the rescue for fear that the helicopter would crash through the trees onto the unsuspecting soldiers directly below him who were preparing their wounded for evacuation. He headed toward Di An, the base camp for the 1st Infantry Division, about four minutes away. He didn't make it. The engine quit seconds after leaving the pick-up zone. Now, Lombard was desperately trying to reach an open area within reach of his glide path. Fortunately, he found one. Directly in front of the doomed helicopter was a decent sized open area in the trees, just big enough to land in. Knowing that he was going down, Lombard told the crew members in the back to brace for a hard landing. With the controls barely working due to a loss of hydraulic fluid, he managed to make a running landing and skidded along the ground to a very rough stop.

By now, flames had engulfed the entire engine compartment and were quickly spreading over the rest of the helicopter. Incredibly, all of the crew managed to get out and were running away from the burning ship when suddenly the medic remembered there were rifles and ammo on board. He dashed back in the burning helicopter, retrieved the M-16s and bandoleers of ammunition, and ran to safety before the helicopter burst into flames.

The euphoria of surviving the crash quickly dissipated as the four men realized that they had overflown the enemy's position while searching for a landing site. Now, the Viet Cong unit that had shot down their aircraft was between them and the US infantry company they were supporting. After a few moments discussion, Lombard and his crew decided that, rather than head into an ambush or fire fight, it was better to head away from the enemy. They began walking toward a knoll in the direction of Long Binh.

However, unknown to Lombard and his small party, a platoon of the infantry company he was supporting was on a sweep operation in the area of the crash and the platoon headed toward the downed aircraft. When Lombard heard them running toward the crash, he and his men hid in the tall grass, ready to open fire on what they believed to be VC. He was about to open fire when he saw they were American soldiers. Lombard and his small group joined the platoon in setting up a defensive perimeter near the crashed helicopter.

Later in the day, the rest of the company finally cut its way out of the jungle and joined them. As dusk approached, a DUST OFF from the 254th flew in and evacuated the wounded along with Lombard and his crew. Unfortunately, the two wounded soldiers Lombard had come for died before they could be evacuated.

In spite of the risks associated with its use, by the end of 1966, the hoist was being used by every DUST OFF unit in the country. As the jungle penetrator became more popular, the use of the vest was, for the most part, discontinued. The rigid lifter was used for patients that were seriously wounded or unconscious.

While the DUST OFF crews were saving lives in the jungle, protests against the war were becoming popular on the home front twelve thousand miles away. This was the year that the war protesters began to get organized, realizing that large demonstrations would attract coverage from the media, thereby greatly increasing the impact of the demonstrations. On the 15th of May, thousands of people marched and chanted in Washington, DC, to protest the deepening American involvement in Vietnam. Most of the protesters were young men of draft age who had a vested interest in the war. They surrounded the White House and vowed to throw congressional supporters of the war out of office. At the University of Chicago, hundreds of draft age students seized the administration building for three days. Most Americans caught up in these protests had no concept of what was going on in Vietnam or even what the issues involved were. In 1966, there was an almost carnival atmosphere surrounding the anti-war demonstrations. American youths were in the midst of a much larger exercise in self expression which included free love, drugs, tattoos, long hair and any other issue that could be used to demonstrate the growing sense of rebellion against any and all authority. The war had not yet captured the nations attention. That would happen in 1968 and it would cost Lyndon Johnson the White House. However, that was still two years in the future. In 1966, America was coping with other problems and social changes. There were other issues, much closer to home, that Americans were focusing on. Race riots rocked Atlanta and Chicago and the miniskirt made its debut. Elvis Presley was competing with the Rolling Stones and the Grateful Dead, and Betty Friedan was trying very hard to make the National Organization for Women into a serious political force. The nation was

Too Late—a dead trooper of the 101st Airborne Division is removed from a DUST OFF at Phan Thiet in May 1966. The mortality rate among the wounded was low. Some 97.5 percent of the wounded who were airlifted from the combat zone survived their wounds.

A helicopter hoist lowers a Stokes rigid litter basket to pick up a wounded man. The litter went into service in 1966 and was used for extracting seriously injured soldiers. However, it was often impossible to lower it through thick, triple-canopy jungles. The Jungle Penetrator soon solved this problem.

going through a dramatic series of social upheavals, some trivial, some not, and Vietnam was a long way off.

Against this backdrop, the US military in Vietnam was desperately trying to save the nation of South Vietnam from communist aggression, and they were doing it with very little support from home. The Johnson administration had allowed the war's critics to steal the agenda concerning Vietnam. This happened, in large part, because the administration had failed miserably in making a strong case for US involvement. This trend would continue until the war ended.

The new year got off to a hectic start very quickly. On January 8th, American forces in the III Corps area launched a major offensive against enemy forces north of Saigon in an area known as the Iron Triangle, near the Cambodian border. Operation Cedar Falls was the largest, most ambitious US operation in the war to date. It involved 20 American and ARVN combat units. During the following 19 days, the units sealed off, searched out, and destroyed enemy complexes, defenses and troop concentrations throughout the area. Nearly a thousand enemy soldiers were killed. DUST OFFs flew around the clock during this period, evacuating hundreds of casualties.

Cedar Falls was a true test of the DUST OFF system. Just as the combat units joined forces in pursuit of a common goal, all of the DUST OFF detachments within flying range of the Iron Triangle supported the operation by coordinating their missions. Requests for DUST OFFs during the operation were funneled through the central dispatch points. This allowed a higher degree of control and eliminated duplication and waste of precious resources. As a result, Cedar Falls received smooth, first-rate DUST OFF coverage.

No matter how many missions were flown, there was never any two exactly the same. Every mission carried the potential for extraordinary events to unfold, both good and bad.

A great deal of the excitement and motivation shared by the DUST OFF crews was the strong desire to make things happen, to be involved in changing the outcome of rapidly developing events. There was also a shared belief that the crews could perform miracles, save lives against all odds, fly through enemy fire without being shot down, and always find room for one more patient. Part of this was the tradition and lore of flying DUST OFFs. It was a proud legacy and the crews were justifiably proud to be a part of it. Another part was the realization of the importance of the work being done. Nothing, absolutely nothing, was more critical or vital. If the crews did not believe each mission carried an opportunity for miracles, they could not fly them with the determination and vigor each mission required. Quite often, the odds were against them. The grim reality was that they could not possibly save every wounded man, yet they had to believe they could. This apparent contradiction was always there, just below the surface. It wasn't often discussed but it was always felt. Miracles, the true kind, were few and far between. What saved most of the wounded was the iron will, skill, and courage of the DUST OFF crews.

Occasionally, however, the DUST OFF crews had the rare opportunity to perform legitimate miracles. One such chance presented itself in late January to Captain Walter Mueller, a DUST OFF pilot with the 498th. On this particular day, Mueller received an urgent request to evacuate a wounded soldier of the 1st Cav from a rice paddy, 20 miles northwest of Nha Trang. The only report Mueller received did not sound encouraging—the soldier was suffering from a sucking chest wound. Experience had taught the DUST OFF pilots that these wounds could be fatal if not quickly treated. If the patient didn't die from loss of blood, then he would die from a lack of oxygen.

It was beginning to get dark when he arrived at the landing zone. The troops on the ground, the ones who had brought the patient to the pick-up point, told Mueller what he didn't want to hear. The man was dead. They explained that he had died shortly after the request for evacuation was made, but there were two other non-urgent casualties and they were loaded aboard.

The man they had come for was lying face down by the edge of the rice paddy, wrapped in a poncho. Mueller was asked to evacuate him also, and he agreed. Sergeant Sullivan, the medic, was loading him aboard when he heard a very faint moan. At first the medic thought the sound was coming from the wind in the trees by the rice paddy. Then he heard it again. This time there was no mistake. The sound was coming from the man he was holding in his arms. Sullivan quickly laid the man on the ground and stripped the poncho from his body. Though seriously wounded, with a large bullet hole in his chest, the man who had been declared dead was very much alive. Immediately, Sullivan got him inside the DUST OFF, bandaged the wound and administered mouth-to-mouth resuscitation, while Mueller made a mad dash for the 8th Field Hospital at Nha Trang. Once airborne, Mueller asked the medic for the mans status.

"He should make it if we hurry," Sullivan answered.

"Then, by God, we'll hurry!" Mueller replied. As Mueller put the RPM gauge in the red zone, the copilot called the 498th to make sure the 8th Field would be ready for them when they arrived. Then he called the Medical Regulating Officer and passed the same urgent message. While this was not exactly routine procedure, sometimes a little redundancy is a good thing. In this case it was both understandable and excusable; they weren't taking any chances on losing their miracle.

This miracle hinged on a number of coincidences happening in the right order. The man had, indeed, stopped breathing while waiting for DUST OFF. Thinking he was dead, his buddies had wrapped him in a poncho and placed him face down on the wet ground. These two actions later proved to be critically important—the poncho and the man's weight, combined with the soft, wet ground, had temporarily sealed the chest wound, allowing him to start breathing again on his own. Had they placed him on his back, he would have died. Had there been a full load of wounded, he would have laid there, by the paddy, until morning, and sometime during the night the little life that was still in him would have seeped out and no would ever know that he could have been saved. Had Sullivan not been so quick and skilled, and had Mueller not been so willing to abuse his aircraft, the wounded man would have died somewhere on the way to Nha Trang.

But this time, it all came together the right way. At Nha Trang, the soldier underwent emergency surgery and, not only survived, but recovered completely. Some days were bet-

(Clockwise from top left) The Jungle Pentrator in Action: Pfc. James Morrison, medic, straps Pfc. John Saphler onto the pentrator...

...and then turns him loose as Saphler is hoisted up...

...to the hovering DUST OFF. As soon as he's aboard...

...SP4 Lonnie Kelly, DUST OFF medic, checks Saphler's wounds and keeps him stable en route to the hospital.

Long Binh, South Vietnam Sergeant Nick Schnieder, squad leader, 199th Light Infantry Brigade, guides a DUST OFF in to evacuate wounded members of his squad.

ter than others. For Mueller, Sullivan, and the rest of the DUST OFF crew, this had been one of the best. One miracle, such as this, could go a long way in offsetting the pain of losing some eighteen year old infantryman because he arrived at the hospital a few minutes too late.

By the middle of 1967, US troop strength in Vietnam was close to 450,000. With the increase in ground forces came an increase in combat, and as combat operations increased, so did casualties. As more and more tactical units arrived in country, more demand was placed on DUST OFF. This was stretching DUST OFF coverage dangerously thin in several areas. To meet this growing burden, General Westmoreland requested four more DUST OFF detachments and an additional DUST OFF company. While the Army fully recognized the urgency and legitimacy of Westmoreland's request, the simple fact was that there was a shortage of medical helicopter units worldwide. The problem was a shortage of helicopters. The only way to quickly increase the number of DUST OFFs was by cutting other airmobile units.

However, there was a way to move more DUST OFFs into the combat zone faster, but it carried with it some risks. If the Army was willing to eliminate unit training before shipping DUST OFF units from the states, then the arrival date of the next DUST OFF company could be accelerated by two months.

Due to the proven accomplishments of the DUST OFF units already in county, the Army decided on the latter course of action, and, on September 13th, the 45th Medical Company, Helicopter Ambulance, became operational at Long Binh. The 45th set up operations next door to the 93d Evacuation Hospital. The arrival of the 45th also marked the beginning of the fourth generation of the Huey in the Vietnam War because the 45th brought with it the latest, most powerful version of the Huey, the UH-1H.

Powered by an AVCO L-13 1,400 horsepower engine, the UH-1H rated 27 percent more horsepower than the L-11 equipped UH-1D, and consumed 9 percent less fuel. This greater fuel efficiency substantially increased the operational radius of the UH-1H. The UH-1H became the latest refinement in a long line of proud achievements from Bell Helicopter. Just as the DUST OFF crews were learning and getting better, so was Bell. Both were striving for, and coming very close to, perfection. With the added power and increased range, it was obvious that other DUST OFF units had to get the UH-1H as soon as possible.

In a desperate attempt to keep up with the rapid build-up in combat forces, the build-up in DUST OFF units continued throughout 1967. The 54th Medical Detachment arrived at Chu Lai, in southern I Corps, and became operational on September the 25th. The mission of the 54th was to support the newly formed Americal Division, the largest division in the US Army at that time.

In October, the 159th Medical Detachment went to work in Cu Chi, 20 kilometers northwest of Saigon. The primary mission of the 159th was to provide direct support to the 25th Infantry Division which was responsible for combat operations in the northwestern portion of III Corps. In November, the 571st Medical Detachment set up shop at Nha Trang, and in December the 50th Medical Detachment arrived at its new home at Phu Hiep in southwest II Corps and assumed responsibility for flying DUST OFFs for the 173d Airborne Brigade, the 28th South Korean Infantry Regiment, and all other friendly units within flying range.

Clearly, the Army was responding to General Westmoreland's request in a timely manner, but none of these units arrived one day too soon. There was tremendous pressure on these new DUST OFF units to get up to speed as quickly as possible. They did not have the luxury of first firmly establishing themselves and then flying missions. In every case, the combat units that these newly arrived DUST OFF detachments were committed to supporting were already on the ground, conducting combat operations. However, the more experienced DUST OFF units pitched in and helped familiarize the new guys, and in a relatively short period of time, the new DUST OFFs were flying like veterans.

As 1967 came to an end, American troop strength in Vietnam had reached 485,000 and was still growing. By this time, the ground combat was in full swing and the five and a half years of experience DUST OFF had accumulated was put to good use. Each generation of DUST OFF crews had added to the sum total of experience acquired, the hard way, of flying the wounded out of harm's way. For the DUST OFFs, 1967 had been the busiest year, by far, to date. Without regard to the enemy, weather, or terrain, 56,378 missions were flown and 98,737 patients were evacuated. The hoist was responsible for 1,372 of these evacuations. Without question, most of these would have died on the jungle floor without this kind of rescue because the hoist offered the only salvation available.

These impressive figures, however, did not come free. Nothing in Vietnam came free. During the course of the year, 40 DUST OFF crewmen were killed, 58 wounded, and 24 helicopters with the big red crosses were lost in the line of duty. These statistics should have come as no surprise to those who truly knew what flying DUST OFF missions was all about. It was about defying the odds and beating them, knowing full well that any mission could very well be the last. It was about looking constantly for the miracle that Mueller found and, if the crew was lucky enough to find it, then it was all worthwhile. The crews tried not to think about the grim reality of the odds they were facing on a daily basis. Rather, they tried to focus on the mission they were flying at the time. Yet the reality was impossible to deny—flying DUST OFFs had become the most dangerous form of flying, by far, in South Vietnam. No amount of technological improvement could alter the basic fact that, in order to accomplish the mission, DUST OFFs had to pick up the wounded in an environment that was so hostile that it had created the casualties. This, by definition, was the most dangerous area in the combat zone. It was a vicious, endless cycle but it continued because it had to. As long as there were wounded on the battlefield, the missions were flown. Chuck Kelly was still riding in the right seat. He didn't have to say anything; his presence was enough.

7

The Tradition Continues
(The Long Day of DUST OFF 55)

During the monsoon season, the mountainous terrain of the southern part of I Corps was often enshrouded in soft, marshmallow clouds several hundred feet thick. What was not covered by the clouds was consumed by the dense ground fog, making it impossible to determine where the clouds ended and the fog began. The clouds and fog alternated with the rain that came down in great, white sheets that swept across the valleys and mountains. During the monsoon season, it was not unusual for the rains to come several times a day.

These were the conditions on January the 5th, 1968, when the 54th Medical Detachment at Chu Lai received a DUST OFF request from a Special Forces camp at Hau Duc. The camp was 25 miles west of Chu Lai in a heavily forested valley surrounded by steep mountains. An enemy force had attacked a South Vietnamese Regional Force patrol shortly after the patrol had left the camp. There were several casualties, including a serious gunshot wound in the abdomen of one of the South Vietnamese soldiers. Sergeant Robert Cashon, the senior medic at the Special Forces camp, patched up the wounded as best he could while waiting for DUST OFF. Conditions more difficult than these would be hard to image, yet the mission was flown.

As darkness approached, a DUST OFF arrived overhead and searched desperately for an opening in the fog. The pilot made several valiant attempts to get to the wounded soldiers on the ground, but finally had to give it up due to the fog and gathering darkness. The pilot simply could not see the ground.

Dawn brought little improvement in the weather—visibility and ceiling were still zero-zero. At first light, another crew made an effort to reach the camp, but they, too, were defeated by the weather.

It was at this point that Major Patrick Brady and his crew volunteered for the mission. With Brady was Lieutenant Foust, copilot, Specialist Brian Browick, crew chief, and Specialist Travis Kanida, medic. Volunteering for this kind of mission was typical of Brady. He had been with Kelly in the Delta, had been there when Kelly was killed, and shared deeply Kelly's philosophy concerning DUST OFFs. In many ways, he was the heir apparent to Kelly—stubborn, head strong, totally committed to getting the job done. No excuses. Fly the mission. Now. Anything else was unacceptable. Now, Brady was on his second tour, flying for the 54th and pushing the DUST OFF tradition. He was also an excellent pilot. Many considered him the best pilot the Army had at this point in time. To those who knew him and had never met Chuck Kelly, Pat Brady was as close as they would ever get to the real thing. Now, they were about to find out just how close to the real thing Pat Brady really was.

Brady and his crew in DUST OFF 55 flew low level just under the cloud base until reaching the mountains, then picked up a trail that wound westward through the mountains to Hau Duc. The fog was so thick that the crew could not see the tips of the helicopters rotor blades, yet Brady kept going. In an attempt to improve visibility, Brady lowered his window and hovered sideways. The rotor blades blew away the fog and allowed Brady to barely make out the trail directly under his skids. While Brady concentrated on the trail, the medic and crew chief peered into the soupy fog looking for trees and mountains. Crawling along above the trail not much faster than any one of them could walk, Brady finally reached the camp and landed between the inner and outer defensive wire—a maneuver than would have been hazardous in perfect weather. The fact that the outpost had taken mortar rounds and was still under sniper fire when DUST OFF 55 touched down only added to the tenseness created by the dense fog. However, the loading of the patients proceeded without incident and, once they were all aboard, Brady made an instrument takeoff, lifting straight up through the fog and flew directly to the hospital at Chu Lai.

A DUST OFF prepares to lift wounded soldiers out of a landing zone in Xa Ba Phuoc Province during Operation Wahiawa, conducted by the 25th Infantry Division northeast of Cu-Chi.

A wounded South Vietnamese scout for the 101st Airborne Division is hoisted up into a DUST OFF. The hoist saved many soldiers from certain death in the dense jungles of South Vietnam.

DUST OFF 55 had just returned to base from the first mission when another mission chattered in over the radio. The crew was still wet with perspiration from the first mission as they crawled back in their Huey. A company of the 198th Light Infantry Brigade, 23d Infantry Division, was in deep trouble on the floor of the Hiep Duc Valley west of Chu Lai. For nine hours, six companies of the 2d North Vietnamese Division rained mortars and rocket fire on the American unit from well dug in and fortified positions in the surrounding hills. The enemy was covering all possible flight paths into the area with 12.7mm antiaircraft guns. Even before Brady got the mission, two aircraft supporting the US forces had been shot down. The zero-weather conditions had already forced one DUST OFF away, which nearly crashed when the pilot and copilot suffered vertigo in the dense fog. Still, there were dozens of casualties waiting for somebody to come and get them and that somebody was Pat Brady. He quickly accepted the mission and this time he took along a medical team to help sort out and stabilize the wounded on the ground.

With the medical team strapped down in the back, Brady cranked up DUST OFF 55 and took off. He flew out several miles from the battle area and found a hole in the soup through which he descended to tree top level. For the second time that day, he hovered sideways along a road and stream which he knew led to the battle area. Although the ship drew fire, the poor visibility and surprise combined to throw off the enemy's aim. Clearly, they were not expecting anyone to be do what Brady was doing.

Agony beyond words—this powerful and emotional photograph was shot through the pilot's window by Capt. Don Retzlaff as he approached the landing zone. "I knew we were too late when I saw the soldier sitting there, arms on knees, looking down at his friend," he said.

When he finally reached the valley floor after twenty long, tense minutes, Brady had the company actually guide the ship in by the sound of the Huey's turbine. Exhibiting total trust in the judgment of the ground unit, Brady drifted left or right depending on what they told him.

Once on the ground, the medical team began a triage operation, separating the wounded by the severity of their injuries. In a matter of minutes, Brady had a full load and the DUST OFF quickly disappeared in a swirling cloud of whiteness. Once safely above the terrain, Brady flew directly to Fire Support Base West and unloaded the patients at the aid station. From there, they would be stabilized and back-hauled to the hospitals. Due to the large number of wounded that still had to be rescued, Brady didn't want to waste any time in getting back to Hiep Duc. Before leaving West, he briefed three other DUST OFF crews on how he would attempt his next mission. The three ships followed Brady as far as they could; however, the thick fog and enemy fire forced them back. Only Brady, in DUST OFF 55, pushed on.

Incredibly, he managed to get in and get out with another load of wounded. Then he did it again. And again. DUST OFF 55 flew four missions into Hiep Duc that day, slowly hovering down the narrow road each time and, each time, drawing more enemy fire. During those four missions, Brady flew 39 men out of the fog shrouded valley of death to safety at Fire Support Base West.

To say that Brady had a successful day would be an understatement. However, his day was far from over. After refueling, DUST OFF 55 was in the air again, responding to an urgent request to evacuate two American soldiers near Phu Nhieu, 14 miles southeast of Chu Lai. Enemy machine-gun fire was sweeping the landing zone when Brady arrived, obviously attempting to wipe out the remaining troops and take out DUST OFF 55 in the process. Brady tried a surprise tactic—he low leveled to the area and dropped in quickly, turning the tail boom of the Huey toward the enemy's heaviest fire. He took heavy fire going in and, once on the ground, the fire intensified. DUST OFF 55 sat there, waiting for the ground unit to load the wounded. However, the enemy fire was so heavy, the ground unit failed to move toward the aircraft.

In the finest tradition of Chuck Kelly, Brady called the ground unit and demanded they give him their wounded. Now, all the elements were in place to repeat that tragic day on July 1st, 1964, when Kelly was killed under identical circumstances. However, this day was different. Brady soon realized that the ground unit was not going to move, so he decided to at least get out of range. As he left the landing zone, he took an intense volley of fire. DUST OFF 55 was hit several times and the controls suffered major damage. Still, Brady refused to leave the area. Hovering out of range, he called the unit again and this time the men on the ground promised to load their wounded if Brady returned. He did, taking fire once again. True to their word, the ground troops loaded their comrades and Brady soon had them in the air conditioned operating suites of the 2d Surgical hospital.

After changing aircraft and getting a relief copilot, Brady was back in the air again, this time in support of another company belonging to the 198th Light Infantry Brigade. The

A casualty is strapped to a penetrator hoist and lifted from the battlefield. The benefits of the hoist were almost incalculable. Without it many soldiers would have died on the battlefield with no way to get them out.

company had been conducting a sweep operation 11 miles southeast of Chu Lai, when the North Vietnamese sprung a carefully laid ambush on one of its platoons. Automatic weapons fire and land mines had killed six members of the platoon and wounded the rest. Brady accepted the mission, even though he was warned to wait until the enemy broke contact. Knowing from experience that waiting on the enemy to do anything could have disastrous results, Brady flew in immediately and landed as close as possible to the wounded, which put him in the middle of a minefield. The wounded were scattered about the battlefield pretty much where they had fallen. The crew chief and medic immediately began loading wounded, disregarding the mines and enemy fire. As they brought one soldier toward the ship, a mine exploded only five yards from the DUST OFF, hurling the three men into the air and ripping hundreds of holes in the helicopters skin. Shaken, but otherwise unhurt, the two crewmen got up and continued the loading. With a full load, Brady made yet another trip to the 2d Surgical at Chu Lai.

Brady had to trade that ship in for another one when he returned to the DUST OFF pad at Chu Lai. He flew two more urgent missions before the long day ended well after dark.

By the end of the day, Brady and his crew had gone through three helicopters that had taken over 400 hits, bullet and shrapnel, from intense enemy action. In the process, Brady evacuated 51 wounded soldiers. This extraordinary performance earned Major Patrick Brady the Congressional Medal of Honor, the first awarded to a DUST OFF crew member. It was only fitting that a protégé of Chuck Kelly was the first of the DUST OFF breed to win this highest honor. However, he would not be the last.

By January 1968, most of the American buildup in Vietnam was complete. During 1968, American military strength in South Vietnam would reach a peak of 536,000. The enemy, frustrated by a series of defeats and the growing American presence, decided it was time to launch an all-out offensive. The North Vietnamese leadership in Hanoi had now become convinced that they could never defeat the forces in the South with protracted "revolutionary" warfare. The war of terror they had waged against the South Vietnamese may have worked before the Americans had arrived in such large numbers, but by early 1968, the North Vietnamese leadership in Hanoi knew they were in real danger of losing the war. The war of attrition was well on the way to being lost by Hanoi. Now, Hanoi was being forced to launch an all out, conventional attack against the Americans and South Vietnamese, or give it up. They could no longer afford to suffer the enormous losses inflicted by superior American fire power day after day. A massive offensive by Hanoi was a gamble and the communist leadership knew it, but they had no alternative. The war was clearly going against them and they had to make an effort to turn it around. The guerrilla war being fought by the Viet Cong was rapidly becoming a failure. Most major Viet Cong units were composed of North Vietnamese regulars and they were being defeated on a regular basis.

For months, Hanoi had carefully planned what the North Vietnamese called the "general uprising." They chose Tet, the Lunar New Year, as the time to strike. Tet had a special significance to the Vietnamese. For years, both sides had observed a truce, or cease fire during this period because celebrating it properly was of profound importance to both sides. It was a time to celebrate and try to forget, for a little while, the war.

On 29 January, 84,000 Viet Cong and North Vietnamese soldiers deliberately violated the traditional Tet cease-fire and launched savage, well coordinated attacks against 36 provincial capitals and over 100 district headquarters. Every major city in the country became a target. The most intense fighting of the war raged throughout the country for 12 days. In the ancient city of Hue, in northern I Corps, the fighting went on for 25 days.

Nothing up to this point in the war provided more of a test to the DUST OFF system than the Tet Offensive. The intense fighting of Tet produced casualties on a massive scale—all over the country. Over 8,000 wounded were evacuated during this 12 day period. Out of a total number of 64 operational DUST OFF helicopters, 40 were hit by enemy fire. Evacuation hospitals near the heaviest fighting were soon full, forcing the DUST OFFs to fly longer evacuation routes. During the first 24 hours of the offensive, the 93d Evacuation Hospital at Long Binh received 215 patients. By February the 8th, the 93d had taken in over 635 and performed over 1,000 major surgeries. In Saigon, which was badly hit, the 57th was evacuating casualties from the streets and flying them to any hospital within range that could take them.

Tet flashed through the Delta with a special intensity. During the first night of fighting, the 82d at Soc Trang lost three DUST OFFs and was forced to borrow replacements from other aviation units. They put them to good use by evacuating 1,400 wounded during the month of February. Throughout the country, DUST OFFs flew around the clock to keep up with demand. The Evacuation and Surgical Hospitals moved the less seriously wounded patients to medical facilities on the coast to clear beds for the critically wounded. The medical staffs in these hospitals also worked around the clock to keep up with the flood of patients. During this period, it was routine for surgeons to work twelve or fourteen hours at a single stretch. After a few hours sleep, they were back in the operating rooms performing major, life saving surgery.

The Viet Cong and North Vietnamese did not limit their assaults to military targets. In Hue alone, over 2,000 civilians were slaughtered and buried in mass graves. Through out the country sides, the communists attacked hamlets and villages suspected of supporting the Saigon government with a special vengeance. Thousands of women, children and old people were brutally murdered to demonstrate what happens to those who refused to support the communists.

When it was over and the smoke cleared, the enemy had suffered a major defeat. The massive, spontaneous general uprising the communist planners had counted on did not happen. Tet proved to be a major military miscalculation for Hanoi. While Tet claimed the lives of 1,001 American soldiers, the enemy lost over 31,000 of its best troops killed in action. DUST OFF made an invaluable contribution by rushing the thousands of casualties to medical facilities, often within minutes of being wounded. DUST OFF had passed the severest test of the war. Never again would the enemy challenge American forces in such large numbers or in such a conventional fashion.

In the aftermath of Tet, the initiative belonged to the Americans and South Vietnamese, and General Westmoreland pleaded with Lyndon Johnson for approval to step up the pace of the war. Johnson, however, chose to read—and believe—the news media's interpretation of Tet which was widely regarded as an American defeat. Tet, more than any other single event, graphically illustrated Johnson's inability to grasp the essential issues of Vietnam. The great irony of the Tet offensive was that it convinced Hanoi that it could never win on military terms against the Americans; it also convinced Johnson, who should have exploited the victory, that he was going to lose. Depressed, delusional, broken and self-absorbed, Johnson finally announced on March 31st that he was no longer a candidate for a second term as president. He chose to take the easy way out of a tragedy of his own making—he simply quit. This, in itself, was no tragedy. The tragedy was it was so late in coming. The war that he never understood finally defeated him because he could not distinguish between defeat and victory.

Despite Johnson's lack of will and commitment to winning, the war continued during 1968. The Tet Offensive had forced several DUST OFF units to move aircraft to other locations around the country in order to keep up with demand. The 498th sent three DUST OFFs to Phu Bai to help with the northern effort. The maintenance units of the 1st Cav agreed to provide support as long as the 498th's aircraft were in the area. These aircraft were still there in early April, providing support to any American unit within flying range.

By now, the North Vietnamese regulars were conducting most of the serious fighting since many of the Viet Cong units had been severely mauled during Tet. The North Vietnamese combat units were usually more aggressive than the VC, better trained and definitely better equipped. As 1968 wore on, the enemy began using more and more sophisticated weapons, including shoulder fired rockets.

Early on the morning of April the 4th, a platoon from the 101st Airborne Division came under an enemy attack while they were still in their night defensive position five miles northeast of Phu Bai. The enemy unit was of unknown size but they were armed with automatic weapons and B-40 rockets fully capable of destroying a tank. It wasn't long before the platoon had casualties—two in critical condition. It was rainy and foggy when the call came for a DUST OFF. The Platoon Leader specified that this mission would require a hoist. At first light, First Lieutenants Michael Meyer and Ben Knisely, on loan to the area from the 498th, accepted the mission.

As soon as they arrived over the area, they set up in high orbit waiting for the escort gunships that were supposed to be coming from Phu Bai. However the gunships couldn't

This is the view many Viet Cong gunners had of DUST OFF in the middle of a hoist mission. These missions required the DUST OFF to assume an absolutely motionless hover while the wounded were hoisted up. Here, a wounded trooper of the 173rd Airborne Brigade is lifted onto a hovering Huey.

get to them due to the fog. At this point, Meyer decided to make a low pass over the area to see if he could make out anything on the ground. In contact all the time with the Platoon Leader of the ground, Meyers was told it probably wasn't a good idea to attempt the hoist mission without gunship protection. The ground unit also told Meyer that this North Vietnamese unit had B-40 rockets. Meyer considered this good advice; he returned to Phu Bai for fuel and the gunship escort.

At noon, they started out again, with the gun ships in tow, to pull the two original casualties. However, by now the ground unit had three more wounded. Once over the area, the gunships made several low passes over the area in an effort to draw fire from the enemy but nothing happened. While they knew the North Vietnamese on the ground were equipped with the B-40 rocket, the helicopter crews did not think the enemy would use it against aircraft since the weapon was designed for ground to ground combat. It had no homing, or seeker, capability. However, the risk that the enemy would take a shot at a hovering helicopter could not be dismissed.

When the gunships drew no reaction, Meyer decided it was time to get on with the hoist operation. He told the ground unit to pop smoke but, due to the extremely heavy canopy, DUST OFF could not see the marker. Meyer settled down closer to the tree trop, hovering only inches above the branches and asked the troops on the ground to do it again. They did. Meyer knew he was close because they could hear him directly overhead. This time, thin threads of purple began to weave upward through the tree tops.

"I identify grape," Meyer told them.

"That's us," the platoon leader replied. "Now I'm going to mark the outside of my perimeter." This was critically important because it would tell the gunships where they could fire if that became necessary. A few seconds later, yellow smoke wafted through the dense canopy thirty yards away. With the ground unit's location now known, Meyer's crew initiated the hoist operation under the watchful eyes of the two gunships hovering nearby, ready to instantly blow great holes in the jungle with the rocket pods strapped to each side of their aircraft. Everybody involved was now on the same frequency. Leaning out of either side of the DUST OFF, the medic and crew chief had considerable difficulty seeing down through the trees. Finally, the medic reported that he could see people on the ground and he started the hoist cable, attached to the jungle penetrator, down through the tree tops.

At this instant, one of the gunship pilots saw a trail of white smoke streaking toward the red cross on the open cargo door of DUST OFF but there was no time to radio a warning. The North Vietnamese had aimed a B-40 rocket at the motionless DUST OFF and pulled the trigger. While not designed as an aintiaircraft weapon, the dumb B-40 was more than capable of blowing anything that could fly out of the sky. The antitank rocket flew through the open door and slammed into the roof of the DUST OFF, directly under the main rotor. The explosion was horrendous. The medic, who was leading out the open cargo door directing the hoist, was immediately blown out of the aircraft. Both Meyer and Knisley instinctively pulled pitch at the same time, trying desperately to save as much rotor speed as they could as the aircraft, now engulfed in flames, half flew and half bounced almost a quarter

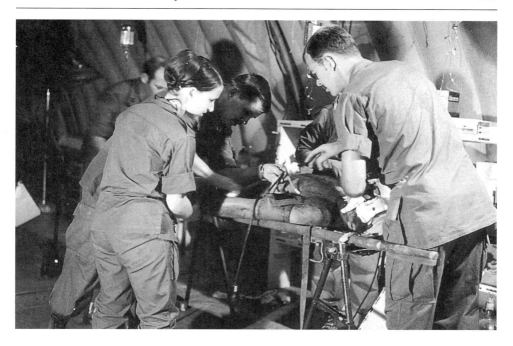

(See above and following) When DUST OFF worked the way it was supposed to, then the surgeons at the evacuation hospitals had a lot of work. The surgeons continued the life saving process that had been started by DUST OFF. The shots illustrate the day to day activity in the evacuation hospitals.

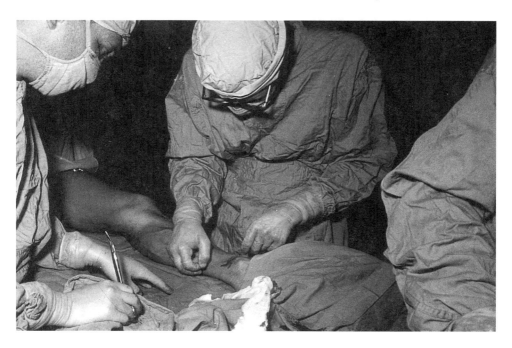

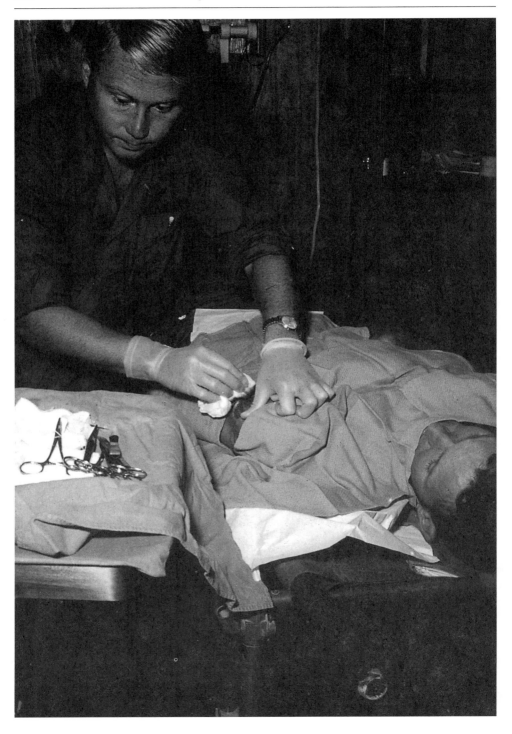

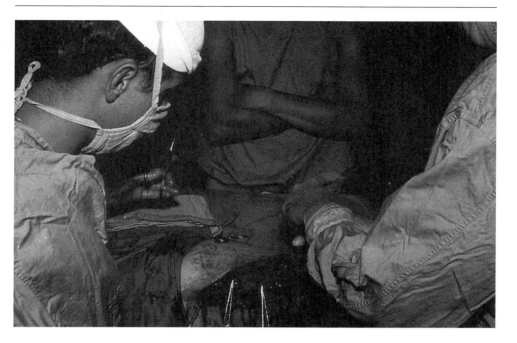

mile down the tree covered mountain side. The last thing Knisley saw was the cargo door flying past his window just before the impact of the blast slammed his head against the door jam. The burning ship crashed through the trees and came to rest on its left side.

Dazed and groggy, Meyer managed to get his door open, crawled up out of the aircraft and dropped to the ground. He ran around to the left side and saw Knisley, unconscious, still strapped in his seat, slumped against the instrument panel. Meyer kicked out the windshield, reached in and unbuckled Knisley. Just then, a fuel cell in the belly of the ship exploded. The impact of the blast knocked Meyer away from the aircraft. However, this didn't stop him; it only slowed him down. Determined to rescue Knisley, Meyer returned and pulled Knisley through the shattered windshield. By this time, Knisley's flight suit was on fire. Meyer patted the flames out with his bare hands and then dragged Knisley a safe distance away. Before he could return to attempt rescuing the crew, the helicopter exploded and was soon completely consumed in a raging inferno of magnesium and fuel.

Meyer pulled the unconscious Knisely into the under brush and waited for a rescue party. About four hours later, Knisely regained consciousness but neither pilot was in any shape to make it out of the area unassisted. Meyer had a broken hand and burns on both his arms. Knisley had third degree burns on his arms and face and a severely broken ankle. There wasn't much they could do other than wait.

Late that afternoon, after hiding in the brush for hours, they heard sounds of someone approaching. Being unarmed and injured, they decided to crawl further into the underbrush and wait. From the voices, the two pilots immediately determined that their approaching visitors were not Americans. Rather, they were North Vietnamese regulars. At the same time the North Vietnamese arrived on the scene, a US rescue party appeared and a fire fight broke out. For a solid twenty minutes, the sharp crack of AK-47s mingled with the sound of M-16s, as bullets whizzed and whined around the smoldering ashes of the dead DUST OFF. Finally, the North Vietnamese broke contact and escaped down the mountain.

With the enemy gone for the moment, Meyer and Knisley heard voices calling out in English. This was the sound Meyer had waited hours to hear, and he answered them. The patrol was from the platoon Meyer and his DUST OFF had come to assist. The platoon leader, his medic, and several members of the platoon had worked their way down the mountain side to the crash site and rescue any survivors. In a reversal of roles that happened quite often in Vietnam, the rescuers were now being rescued. They had fully expected to run into the North Vietnamese; however they did not expect to encounter them at the site of the crash. It had taken the rescue party over four hours to work their way to the crash site, which clearly illustrates how rugged this piece of terrain was.

After the medic checked out the two pilots and did what he could for them, they began the long, tortuous trip back up the mountain to the platoon's defensive position. Knisely, only intermittently conscious, could not walk and had to be carried or dragged. They only made a few hundred meters that first night. As they settled into the hastily prepared overnight position, Meyer and Knisely discussed the loss of their crew chief and medic. The four man crew had been close and the loss of the two men who worked the back of the DUST OFF was keenly felt.

The next morning, just after dawn, the small party once again attacked the mountain. After about an hour of steady climbing, pulling, carrying and dragging, the small group took a rest break. That's when they heard someone shouting. It sounded like it was coming from the trees above them. Someone was calling out in English from the tree tops! They looked up and finally saw where the sound was coming from. The medic, who had been blown out of the DUST OFF by the B-40 rocket the day before, had landed in the trees. After realizing that their medic was alive, Meyer and Knisely were overjoyed. The troops from the platoon managed to get him down, discovering, in the process, that he had a broken hip and various bruises and contusions. All in all, however, he was one very lucky guy, considering that he been blown out of a helicopter by an enemy rocket. This miracle helped to ease the pain of losing the crew chief, who perished in the inferno at the crash site.

Early that afternoon, the rescue party and the three survivors rejoined the platoon where they learned that the more serious gunshot victims—the ones that DUST OFF had been trying to save the day before—had died. With any sense of urgency now gone, and considering that the enemy was still active and present in the area, the downed crew told the ships overhead that there was no real necessity in getting in and they spent a second night on the ground with their rescuers.

The next morning, Meyer, Knisely, the medic and the three wounded troopers from the platoon were hoisted out of the jungle and flown to the hospital.

Throughout the remainder of 1968, DUST OFF missions increased dramatically as the US forces applied maximum pressure on the enemy. During this year, over 200,000 wounded were evacuated under increasingly hazardous circumstances. Of that number, nearly 2,000 were picked up by hoist, which was, by far, the most dangerous evacuation technique. It took 56,378 missions to accomplish this incredible feat. The new UH-1H played a major role in the success of the DUST OFF program. By now, every evacuation unit was flying the H model.

Another contributing factor to the success achieved was the experience of the crews. Most of the pilots were on their second tour and some were on their third. This kind of experience added a special stability and maturity to DUST OFF. The experience gained on previous tours was passed on to the younger pilots and the whole system benefited. The legend of Chuck Kelly was very much alive and well.

While the Americans were making great progress in destroying the enemy's main force units on the battlefield, the war was not going very well on the home front. This was a year of turmoil for America. Martin Luther King and Robert Kennedy were both killed and race riots ripped through Americas major cities. On top of this, the nation was also plagued with countless anti-war demonstrations, which seemed to reach a zenith with the Democratic National Convention in Chicago. A kind of bizarre, self-destructive behavior seemed to

Members of the 4th Bn., 173d Airborne Bde, load their wounded on Hill 875 in November 1967. The battle for Hill 875 was one of the fiercest engagements of the war. Over four days and nights US units fought to dislodge North Vietnamese troops in bunkers who had used their entrenched positions to launch mass attacks on US troops around Dak To in the Central Highlands.

possess thousands of Americans during this period. It seemed that throughout 1968, just about any event was justification for a riot. None of it had to make sense; all that mattered was the crowd attracted by the event.

Finally, the Vietnam War was receiving a great deal of attention at home, and most of it was bad. In fact, the Vietnam War was the deciding factor in the presidential election that year. Hubert Humphery, hopelessly tainted by his close association with the ineffectual Lyndon Johnson, lost by a landslide to Richard Nixon. Nixon promised to end the war with honor, and a clear majority of Americans believed him and, because they did, they made him president. The war was about to enter a new phase, under new leadership.

8

1969
(Year of Change)

Richard Nixon inherited all the negatives Vietnam produced when he was sworn in as president in January, 1969. Since Johnson had squandered so much time and so many opportunities to win, Nixon had very little left to work with. However, unlike Johnson, Nixon actually had a strategy that would ensure a democratic South Vietnam. During the last months of the Johnson administration, the North Vietnamese refused to make any concessions at the peace talks in Paris simply because they knew they didn't have to. Nixon was different. He was prepared to hammer the North Vietnamese into submission, if necessary, to get them to the peace table.

A DUST OFF hovers on a helipad of a makeshift hospital ship in the Delta after rescuing wounded members of the Riverine Force. Aside from the wounded, scores of riverine troops had to be treated for "Immersion foot"—a fungal infection caused by prolonged exposure to swamp water. It was overcome by rotating units so that the men periodically had a chance to "dry out."

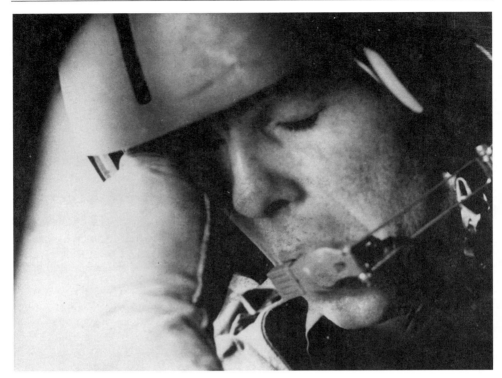

Signs of strain and exhaustion are etched on the face of a DUST OFF crew member after a long mission. Dedication to bringing out the wounded was paramount and crews often resented regulations that kept them, in their view, unnecessarily grounded. Consequently, crews frequently flew many more hours than they logged.

Nixon, however, had an enemy on the home front that Johnson didn't have—the US congress. Mostly democratic and still smarting from the Republican presidential victory, the democrats in congress were reluctant to grant Nixon's wishes regarding the war, even if he succeeded in bringing Americans home and securing freedom for South Vietnam. In 1969, many congressmen had little stomach for defending Vietnam, since to do so was becoming a political liability. The victory Johnson had promised so many times didn't happen; why should they support Nixon's strategy? And, if Nixon actually managed to do what Johnson failed to do, it would make democrats look weak and ineffectual. Thus, Nixon's strongest enemies were far removed from the combat zone, sitting safely on capitol hill.

In the truest sense of the word, the Vietnam war had now become political. Still, Nixon was determined to end the war on terms the American people could accept, in spite of the democratic congress. His overall objective was to make the North Vietnamese believe it was in their best interest to negotiate an end to the war and, at the same time, turn more and more of the fighting in the south over to the South Vietnamese. This would allow an orderly, withdrawal of American units. This program was called "Vietnamization," and, to a large degree, it was successful.

To the US units in the field, the change in administrations made little, if any, difference in the daily routine of combat operations. The sweep operations continued and the DUST OFFs kept flying in a seemingly endless cycle.

In early 1969, Captain Don Retzlaff was back in country again, flying with the 498th for the second time. On a bright, sunny day in late February, he and his crew were called on to join the search for a DUST OFF that had crashed near An Khe the night before. They soon found the burned-out hulk of the aircraft on the side of a densely forested mountain. Unable to land, Retzlaff hovered over the wreck while his medic descended on the hoist to inspect the crash site. After carefully inspecting the wreckage, the medic was hauled up. He reported that the destruction was so complete, it was impossible to determine if there were survivors. It certainly did not look good for the crew of the downed DUST OFF, but Retzlaff was not about to give up. DUST OFF crews were special, particularly to other DUST OFF crews. So, Retzlaff continued to search the area, hovering over the jungle, searching for some glimmer of hope that there was survivors on the ground. After nearly an hour of this, even Retzlaff was beginning to lose hope of finding anyone alive, yet he was still unwilling to give up. They were about a half a mile from the crash site when Retzlaff saw it—the top of one of the trees was moving! Thinking the movement was caused by the prop wash, Retzlaff hovered away, still keeping his eyes glued to this particular treetop. He wanted to be absolutely certain before he told the crew. When it moved again, with the helicopter

While most of DUST OFF's pick-ups were on land, occasionally an airman would be plucked out of the South China Sea off the coast of Vietnam.

hovering at a distance, Retzlaff began to get excited. He positioned the aircraft directly over the tree and peered down through a tiny opening in the lush, green carpet. There, on the ground, over 60 feet below the hovering DUST OFF, he saw the two pilots vigorously shaking the tree trunk. The jungle penetrator was quickly lowered and the two grateful pilots were hoisted up. The unorthodox signaling technique, combined with Retzlaff's experience, determination and instincts, had worked. Suffering only minor wounds, the two extremely lucky pilots were back flying in a couple of days.

While it may not have been obvious to the units fighting the war, 1969 was definitely a year of change. In Paris, the peace talks, which had begun after the Tet Offensive the year before, began concentrating on substantive issues. In March, US forces reached a peak level of 541,000. This would prove to be the largest number of American forces in Vietnam. This level, however, would not be maintained for long. In June, the Nixon administration announced that US troops would be withdrawn in phases and the Vietnamese would pick up a larger burden of the war.

The new buzz word, Vietnamization, was being used more and more now. Back in the states, the war protesters were putting pressure on the new administration to end the war as quickly as possible, regardless of the outcome. Nixon had no intention of running out on the South Vietnamese; however, he knew that American troops had to be withdrawn since this was one of the center pieces of his campaign. In the Pentagon and Saigon, endless strategy sessions were held in an attempt to determine the best political and military policies that should be pursued.

A crew chief peers out the open cargo door of a DUST OFF, keeping a steady eye on the wounded soldier being hoisted up on a rigid stretcher.

While there may have been confusion and self doubt at the top of the government, it did not carry down to the DUST OFF units. While other men far away negotiated South Vietnam's future, the men responsible for rescuing the wounded continued to perfect their dangerous art. DUST OFF was about to win another Medal of Honor, even as the troop drawdown got under way.

On the afternoon of October 2d, 1969, the 82d Medical Detachment at Soc Trang received a request for

DUST OFF from a Vietnamese unit on the Cambodian border in Kien Tuong Province. Early that morning, three South Vietnamese companies had stumbled into a VC training camp, complete with well-fortified bunkers. Most of the uninjured soldiers had managed to get through the swamps and rice paddies to safety, but others could not get out and the

A soldier waits patiently for a DUST OFF with his burnt hands bandaged after dry grass was set alight by M-60 machine gun fire.

enemy was laying down a deadly field of fire against the men in the paddies. The battle had been raging for hours before DUST OFF was called. The South Vietnamese Air Force had used napalm on the enemy positions but it did not keep the VC from firing on the injured men in the swamps and rice paddies. Now, it was simply a matter of time before the VC killed all the men in front of them.

Chief Warrant Officer Michael J. Novosel accepted the mission, although he and his crew had already flown seven hours that day. Novosel, 48 years old, was on his second tour of duty. A World War II combat aviation veteran who had piloted B-29s in bombing raids over Tokyo, he had given up a lucrative career as a commercial airline pilot to fly DUST OFFs. When the Vietnam War began to heat up in the early 60s, Novosel decided he would see if the military could use his services. As a lieutenant colonel in the Air Force reserves, he applied for a flying assignment with the US Air Force. However, he was told that the Air Force was over strength in the senior grades, and they turned him down. Undeterred, Novosel offered his considerable experience to the US Army. The Army took him and offered him a Warrant. Novosel accepted and pulled his first tour of duty in 1966 where, as a DUST OFF pilot, he evacuated over 2,000 wounded. Now, he was back for his second tour because he thought he could be of help.

After the carnage—The wounded are loaded aboard at Hamburger Hill, May 1969.

At five feet four inches and 150 pounds, he was hardly the stereotype of a combat pilot. In fact, due to glaucoma, which he treated himself four times a day, the soft spoken Novosel had to get a waiver from the Army to be flying at all. He got the waiver and he was doing what he loved best—flying.

Upon receiving the call, Novosel, who was airborne at the time, headed immediately for the border. To reach the mission site, DUST OFF 88 flew through a series of rain and thunderstorms, but broke into the clear several minutes before reaching the area. It had taken him forty minutes to reach the battle area. Along with Novosel aboard DUST OFF 88 was Warrant Officer Tyrone Chamberlain, copilot, Specialist Fourth Class Herbert Heinold, medic, and Specialist Forth Class Joseph Horvath, crew chief. Also on the scene was a command and control helicopter piloted by Captain Harry Purdy. Purdy briefed Novosel and his crew on the tactical situation and it did not sound good. There were several isolated groups and singles of South Vietnamese scattered throughout the tall grass in and around the paddies. All communications had been lost with the Vietnamese troops on the ground. There was an unknown number of dead and wounded in the area; no body knew exactly how many. As if this news wasn't bad enough, Purdy had one final bit of really bad news for Novosel—the gunships that had been on station earlier had left to rearm and refuel and it would be some time before they returned. Novosel thanked Purdy for the briefing and then decided to go in low and take a close look for himself.

Novosel made two approaches over the battle area but none of the wounded was visible. Enemy fire was keeping them low in the tall grass. Since he had no radio contact with the beleaguered troops, Novosel circled at a safer range, allowing them to see him. Finally, one soldier stood up and waved his shirt. DUST OFF 88 dropped down beside him and the crew pulled him aboard. Once again, Novosel pulled up, circled, and waited for more. By ones and twos, the Vietnamese soldiers waved from the tall grass and Novosel picked them up, right in front of the VC gunners. On one single approach, the crew pulled four aboard. At least one soldier was killed while waving for pick-up.

With a full load, Novosel flew to the Special Forces camp at Moc Hoa, unloaded the wounded, refueled and headed back. While Chamberlain monitored the instruments and looked for wounded, Horvath and Heinold hung out either side of the aircraft on the skids and pulled the wounded inside. Where the grass was too tall to land, they hung onto litter straps and reached down into the deep grass for the casualties. DUST OFF 88 was taking a lot of hits in the process and some of them were doing real damage. The radio and most of the instruments were shot away and the transmission had taken some rounds as well.

With a second load, Novosel flew to Moc Hoa while the crew in the back treated the wounded. Once on the ground at the special forces camp, Novosel got out and took a close look at DUST OFF 88. The main rotor had been hit several times and hydraulic fluid was leaking from more places than Novosel wanted to think about, but he headed back for a third load. On that trip, with nine wounded already on board, Horvath spotted a wounded soldier near one of the bunkers. In an effort to protect the ship and crew from the enemy inside the bunker, Novosel hovered backward toward the man and, as soon as he could

Medal of Honor: Chief Warrant Officer Michael J. Novosel, the second DUST OFF pilot to receive the Medal of Honor. Novosel was awarded the nation's highest military award for his extraordinary and courageous actions on 2 October 1969 near the Cambodian border in Kien Tuong Province.

reach him, Horvath grabbed his arm and started pulling him inside. Suddenly, a VC stood up in the grass directly in front of DUST OFF 88 and opened fire at point blank range. AK-47 slugs shattered the windshield. Shrapnel and pieces of Plexiglas buried deep in Novosel's right calf and thigh. Fragments from the windshield tore into his right hand.

"Ah, hell. I'm hit!" he shouted to Chamberlain as the aircraft instantly leaped 60 feet into the air. In the back, Horvath somehow managed to hang onto the wounded Vietnamese, who was dangling out of the open cargo door, and finally pulled him in. Novosel and Chamberlain quickly regained control and flew out of the area under withering enemy fire.

When it was all over, DUST OFF 88 had put in eleven hours of hard flying that day. Novosel and his crew made three round trips to the Moc Hoa camp and at least fifteen sorties into and around the enemy training area. As a result of their efforts, 29 South Vietnamese soldiers were rescued, most of them seriously wounded, and Michael Novosel became the second DUST OFF Medal of Honor winner. He was also the oldest winner the Vietnam War produced. All of this from a man who just wanted to be of some help. The Kelly legacy was still growing.

The fact that this VC training center was located on the Cambodian border was no accident. The North Vietnamese and Viet Cong were becoming more and more concerned about the increased aggressiveness of American and South Vietnamese operations. And the enemy was taking horrendous losses. As 1969 wore on, the enemy began moving more and more supplies and weapons into what he considered to be sanctuaries inside Cambodia and Laos. From these safe havens, the enemy would then launch attacks across the border into South Vietnam. During the Johnson years, American military forces had been forbidden to cross the border in pursuit of the enemy. Johnson was fearful that such actions would widen the war. Richard Nixon had no such fears or allusions. Before 1969 came to a close, the top military leaders of the US military had begun to secretly plan an attack into Cambodia, designed to strip the enemy of his safe havens and speed the end of the war.

As 1969 came to a close, the DUST OFF crews had every right to feel proud. The figures compiled were staggering by any measurement. They flew 120,841 missions and evacuated 241,151 wounded. The cost, however, had been high—37 crewmen killed, 138 wounded, and 61 aircraft lost.

9

The Price of Life
(Rescues in Cambodia and Laos)

For many years prior to 1970, the US military planners had been frustrated by the enemy simply crossing the border into Cambodia in order to evade allied troops. Strikes on enemy sanctuaries had long been advocated by the military leadership but these requests had been routinely turned down by the Johnson administration. This had been one of the most irritating and frustrating issues that General Westmoreland had been forced to deal with. Now, in early 1970, things were much different. General Westmoreland had been replaced by General Creighton Abrams. Abrams was determined to smash enemy base camps in Cambodia and even Laos. As it turned out, events in early 1970 were making this more likely than ever. Not only was Nixon more aggressive than Johnson had been, now things were taking a turn for the better in Cambodia. In February, the pro-western military leader, Lieutenant General Lon Nol, led a successful coup d' etat against the pro-Communist leader, Prince Norodom Sihanouk. Sihanouk had allowed the North Vietnamese and Viet Cong to have a free hand in operations in Cambodia. As a result, the communists knew that they could store weapons and supplies safely in Cambodia. For years, Cambodia had been used as a staging area for attacks against South Vietnam.

Shortly after taking power, Lon Nol issued an ultimatum setting March the 18th as the closure date of Cambodia's borders to North Vietnamese and Viet Cong forces. The North Vietnamese retaliated by intensifying their incitement of the Cambodian communists, the Khmer Rouge, to conduct attacks against the Cambodian government. Now, finally, US forces would be allowed to pursue the enemy into what had been a protected area—Cambodia. Abrams, however, was not content to simply limit cross-border attacks to Cambodia. He wanted to chase the enemy into Laos as well, but Laos would have to wait. By 1970, the enemy had virtually given up on achieving any kind of victory brought about by guerrilla warfare. The people had failed to support the communists and now Hanoi realized that the communist forces were again in real danger of losing the war. The home grown Viet Cong military units were lying in shreds all over the country. Clearly, the communists' war of liberation was a dismal failure. Without a massive and constant infusion of fresh troops from the North, there would no longer be a war and Hanoi was painfully aware of this. Having virtually given up on a military victory in the South, Hanoi was content to occupy as much of the South as they could, hoping for a favorable settlement from the peace talks in Paris. The North Vietnamese strategy was to occupy as much of South Vietnam as possible when the war ended.

General Abrams, however, had another view. His goal was to hammer the enemy into submission and force North Vietnam to withdraw from all of South Vietnam. Abrams was different than Westmoreland. He wasn't much of a statesman or diplomat. Unlike the tall, distinguished looking Westmoreland, Abrams appearance was somewhat rumpled and untailored. However, he was a soldiers' soldier and he had no allusions about his mission. Abrams was after a military victory. Leaving politics to those in Saigon and Washington, Abrams wanted to clear the battlefield of all enemy resistance. If that meant driving deep into Cambodia and even Laos, then that was what he would do. Finally, after years of American involvement in Vietnam with weak leadership in the White House, Abrams now had a Commander in Chief in Washington who was willing to gamble on winning instead of simply not losing.

For months, MACV had been secretly planning to launch an offensive across the border of Cambodia. After several briefings on the importance of these operations, President Nixon gave his final approval on April the 28th. However, due to intense political opposition Nixon knew he would receive on the home front, he set a deadline of the 28th of June for all US forces to be out of Cambodia.

On the morning of May 1st, elements of several US combat units—the 1st Infantry Division, the 1st Cav, the 25th Infantry Division, and the 11th Armored Cavalry Regiment, along with several South Vietnamese units—crossed the border and struck enemy base camps northwest of Saigon in an area known as the Parrot's Beak. DUST OFF supported both South Vietnamese and American troops in this operation.

During the two months of intense fighting, DUST OFFs evacuated over 11,000 wounded under some of the most difficult conditions imaginable. Although constituting only eight percent of the total missions for May, hoist missions accounted for over fifty percent of the ships hit by enemy fire during that month. In May, 15 DUST OFFs were hit, 4 shot down, 11 severely damaged, 10 crewmen wounded and one killed. At one point in the invasion, over twenty battles were raging along the entire length of the border.

But the success of the operations across the border far exceeded expectations. Thousands of tons of weapons, ammunition and supplies were captured, forcing the enemy to give up a planned spring-summer offensive against the US and South Vietnamese forces in the South. The surprise and intensity of the cross-border attack caught the North Vietnamese by surprise. Many enemy units simply retreated deeper into Cambodia, leaving their supplies unguarded.

Against the larger backdrop of the overall operation, individual acts of heroism and courage stand out as stark reminders of the personal sacrifice combat often demands.

On May the 24th, in the midst of the invasion, a MEDEVAC of the 1st Cav's Air Ambulance Platoon responded to a request from a South Vietnamese unit five miles deep in Cambodia, across the border from Tay Ninh Province. The mission went to 1st Lieutenant

Stephen Modica, commander of MEDEVAC 2, and his crew. MEDEVAC 2 was at Phuoc Vinh, having just replaced both rotor blades that had been shot up the day before. Modica and the crew were preparing to fly back to their stand-by position at Katum when the call came in. In fact, the crew just finished loading beer and soda for the advisors at Katum when they received the call. The beverages were quickly off loaded onto the landing pad and DUST OFF 2 was airborne.

As Modica and his co-pilot, 1st Lieutenant Leroy Canberreaux, eased the aircraft into the landing zone, they came under heavy North Vietnamese fire from gunners hidden in the tree line. Even though there were two Cobra gunships on station suppressing the enemy fire, the enemy kept firing. The pilot of one of the Cobras radioed Modica that they were taking fire, but Modica replied that the wounded had to get out. Seconds later, the North Vietnamese gunners directed a savage volley of fire at MEDEVAC 2. Two slugs tore into Modica's flack jacket and a third ripped through his left knee.

The aircraft slammed down hard, causing Canberreaux to turn to Modica and jestfully suggest that he needed more practice. At that instant, Canberreaux saw the reason for the rough landing—blood was spurting from Modica's shattered left leg. Immediately, the co-pilot took the controls and pulled the aircraft out of the landing zone. MEDEVAC 2 shot fifty feet into the air when the enemy unleashed another vicious barrage of fire from the tree line. The enemy fire knocked out the engine and shot away the tail boom, causing the helicopter to crash back to the ground and roll over on its side.

The two gunships overhead made low firing passes at the enemy in order to give the crew a chance to get out. At this point, the Cobra pilots didn't know if any one was alive on MEDEVAC 2. Lieutenant George Alexander, piloting one of the gunships, put out an urgent Mayday for the downed aircraft and then called MEDEVAC Operations and gave the location of Modica's helicopter. Alexander's Cobra took 29 hits before he expended all his ammunition and had to depart the area.

On board the downed aircraft, all the crew members were stunned at first and unable to move. By chance, Staff Sergeant Louis R. Rocco, a medic who was an advisor to the South Vietnamese, was on board MEDEVAC 2. He was hitching a ride from Phuoc Vinh back to his unit when MEDEVAC 2 received the mission. Rocco asked Modica if he could go along and Modica said yes. Now, Rocco was on the ground, deep inside Cambodia, with the crew of MEDEVAC 2, and it did not look good for any of them.

The impact of the crash threw Rocco from the aircraft, broke his hip and wrist, and severely bruised his back, and knocked him unconscious. When he came to, Rocco quickly realized that the crew was still trapped in the now burning helicopter. With total disregard for the enemy fire or his own injuries, Rocco pulled Modica through the shattered windshield and half carried, half dragged the wounded pilot across 20 meters of exposed terrain to the perimeter of the South Vietnamese forces. Then he went back for Canberreaux, who had a broken collar bone and fractured ribs. As Rocco dragged the injured copilot toward the perimeter, two bullets hit Canberreaux in his flack jacket. Knowing that the medic and crew chief were still in the burning helicopter, Rocco tried to get the South Vietnamese to help him. However, they refused because the North Vietnamese were still laying down a heavy rate of fire at anyone who moved. Determined to do all he could, Rocco went back once again to the burning wreck. This time, he found the medic, Specialist Terry Burdette. Burdette had a broken shoulder and a broken leg.

Rocco pulled Burdette across the open ground to safety also, but he moved slower now because the pain of his own injuries was beginning to kick in.

When he got Burdette to the relative safety of the South Vietnamese perimeter, Rocco realized that the door gunner, Specialist Gary Taylor was still in the wreck. Now he made his fourth trip across the open ground, crawling slower now because of the pain in his hip. The North Vietnamese gunners crewed up the soft ground all around him, throwing dirt in his face and eyes. Still, he pressed on, determined to get Taylor. Taylor was dead, crushed by the helicopter when it rolled over on its side, but Rocco had no way of knowing this. He severely burned both hands, searching blindly in the smoke and flame filled wreckage, before he was finally forced to give up and crawl back to the perimeter.

Having saved all the survivors of MEDEVAC 2, Rocco proceeded to treat their injuries as well as those of the wounded South Vietnamese that MEDEVAC 2 had come for. There was very little he could do for the pain of the wounded, including himself. There was no morphine, so the wounded were forced to suffer. Finally, during the night, Rocco's fractured hip stiffened and the excruciating pain caused him to collapse.

During the long hours of darkness, the enemy launched three attacks on the tiny perimeter. Each time, the attacks were repelled by gunships and artillery fire. Finally, the next

This is an artist's impression of a DUST OFF approaching a landing zone.

morning, an artillery barrage of smoke rounds provided a screen for DUST OFFs, allowing them to rescue the wounded. One DUST OFF was hit by an enemy rocket, but the crew managed to bring the ship down without further casualties and they were soon rescued.

Sergeant Rocco's extraordinary actions that day, five miles inside Cambodia, earned him the Congressional Medal of Honor. "His bravery under fire," stated the citation, "and intense devotion to duty were directly responsible for saving three of his fellow soldiers from certain death."

Without question, the attacks into Cambodia were unqualified successes. Although the enemy resistance never equaled predictions, the amount of weapons and material captured far surpassed what was expected from the operations planners.

While the invasion in Cambodia was a tremendous morale booster for the allies, 1970 also revealed some serious shortcomings on the part of the South Vietnamese military. One of the key deficiencies was a dedicated DUST OFF capability. Several efforts had been made over the years to get the South Vietnamese into the DUST OFF business, but nothing of any significance had actually happened. As long as the US Army's DUST OFF assets could carry the load, then this had not been a critical issue. Now, however, it had to be addressed and some changes needed to be made if the Vietnamization Program, being pushed by the American government, was going to succeed. By now, the numbers were beginning to force policy changes. For example, during the first 11 months of 1970, over 100,000 South Vietnamese patients had been flown to medical stations. This number represented 62% of the total patient load of DUST OFF. Clearly, the time had come to involve South Vietnamese pilots in the evacuation business. While the South Vietnamese Air Force was not eager to fly DUST OFF missions, not all the blame could be placed on them. Ironically, it was the US Air Force that proved to be an obstacle in 1970. The US Air Force, which was the principal advisor and supporter to the South Vietnamese Air Force, had gone on record as being opposed to the creation of dedicated DUST OFF units as "ridiculous and a waste of assets." This attitude was about to change. Before the year ended, the South Vietnamese Air Force had selected two squadrons that would be converted to flying DUST OFFs and nothing else.

As a result of the tremendous success in Cambodia in 1970, American and Vietnamese commanders began detailed planning for a major attack on the enemy's base camps in Laos. Intelligence reports indicated that the North Vietnamese were preparing for a major spring-summer offensive in 1971, and that this attack would be staged from Laos. By October, 1970, allied assessments of all intelligence data indicated two very disturbing phenomena. After recovering from the tremendous setbacks inflicted by the May-June allied invasion of Cambodia, the enemy intended to strangle Phnom Penh, capital of Cambodia and depose the Lon Nol government. Secondly, the North Vietnamese were improving their road networks, building supply reserves, and conducting reinforcement operations in preparation for large scale offensive operations in I Corps.

It was now time to initiate Operation Lam Son 719. Lam Son, meaning "sure win" was designed to strike the enemy's war fighting capability in Laos before he was able to attack allied units in South Vietnam. The success of the Cambodian operation the year before had convinced the American and South Vietnamese leadership that the way to be effective was to deny the enemy any safe refuge. Lam Son 719 was designed to take the refuge of Laos away from the North Vietnamese.

Beginning on February the 8th and continuing to April the 9th, US aircraft transported South Vietnamese troops into Laos, gave them massive fire support, and evacuated their wounded and dead. Some 650 US Army helicopters supported this operation, which involved 42 South Vietnamese maneuver battalions. However, unlike the Cambodian invasion, American combat units were not allowed to enter Laos.

Laos turned out to be DUST OFFs greatest challenge in the Vietnam War. The complexity and character of the operation presented an endless number of problems. Without US forces on the ground in the combat area, communications became a serious problem. Transporting large numbers of wounded in a rapidly changing tactical environment presented other dilemmas. While President Nixon had placed a ban on US combat units in Laos, this ban did not cover DUST OFFs, since they were considered non-combatants. Without Americans on the ground to give concise, reliable instructions to the DUST OFF pilots, the stage was now set for a brutal test of the abilities of the DUST OFF crews. Add to this explosive situation the fact that the enemy had built the most extensive antiaircraft system of the war in Laos and the true dimensions of what faced these DUST OFF crews becomes crystal clear.

The North Vietnamese had deployed this extensive antiaircraft capability in the rugged mountainous terrain of Laos. It was well integrated and mobile. Many of these antiaircraft weapons were radar controlled missiles. In addition to the missiles, the enemy had deployed over 750 medium caliber antiaircraft machine guns throughout the operational area, which were moved daily. This made their detection and destruction an almost impossible task. Almost every potential landing zone inside Laos was covered with mortar, artillery, and rocket fire. All DUST OFF missions were required to run this deadly gauntlet to get out the wounded, often without gunship escorts. Yet, in the face of these impossible obstacles, 6,632 wounded were evacuated during Lam Son 719.

When it was over, it became painfully obvious that the South Vietnamese armed forces were not yet prepared to go on the offensive alone against the better equipped North Vietnamese main force units. The sad reality was that the South Vietnamese lacked the leadership to deal the enemy a decisive defeat. In the end, Lam Son 719 accomplished one major objective—it delayed a major offensive for several months. However, those who expected a repeat of the spectacular success achieved in Cambodia were disappointed.

Still, Laos added to the proud legacy of DUST OFF. On February the 18th, a DUST OFF from the 237th Medical Detachment was shot down as it attempted to leave a fire support base 9 kilometers inside Laos, wounding the crew. Under heavy enemy fire, another DUST OFF landed and evacuated all members of the downed helicopter crew except the crew chief, Specialist 4 Dennis M. Fujii. Suffering from shrapnel wounds in the back and shoulder, Fujii was pinned down near a bunker by a heavy mortar barrage. As the second DUST OFF made repeated attempts to get closer to the crew chief, Fujii waved off his rescuers due to the intense enemy fire. Finally, the DUST OFF was forced away, leaving Fujii, the only American soldier on the ground in Laos, surrounded by two North Vietnamese regiments.

Enemy gunners kept up their near continuous deluge of rockets, mortars and small arms fire. At about 4:30 that afternoon, Fujii found an operational PRC-25 radio and began broadcasting with the call sign "Papa Whiskey." He told the pilots high overhead that he wanted no more attempts to pull him out because the landing zone was too hot.

For the rest of that day and much of the next, Fujii put his six months of cross training as a medic with DUST OFF to good use and bandaged up the South Vietnamese wounded on the fire support base.

At about 9:30 PM, the 102d North Vietnamese Regiment, supported by heavy artillery, began a ground attack on the small base. Twice that night, the enemy penetrated the perimeter before being repulsed. At one point, North Vietnamese troops massed near the old eastern outpost, preparing for a massive attack. Considering the number of enemy troops involved, the attack would have definitely overrun the support base. Fujii, observing what was taking place, radioed the aircraft overhead and called for an immediate airstrike on the

Medics at the 71st Evacuation Hospital wait at the helipad for a DUST OFF to touch down and land the wounded from the Cambodian combat zone. Within minutes of landing the patients would be sorted according to surgical priority and given treatment.

enemy. F-4 Phantoms streaked in and dropped 1,000 pound bombs. C-130 gunships laid down withering ropes of fire only twenty meters from the friendly positions. The enemy assault was broken up before it began.

However, the ordeal was far from over. For seventeen hours, Fujii remained on the air, calling in and adjusting friendly fire as the enemy made several desperate attempts to wipe out Fujii and the South Vietnamese troops. From 9:30 PM on the 19th through 7:30 AM on the 20th, Fujii worked with the forward air controllers, coordinating flare ships and gunships that worked throughout the night to keep the North Vietnamese at bay. Papa Whiskey was silent only when he had to trade his radio for an M-16 to fight off the attackers. During the night, Fujii directed several precision aerial bombardments that came within a few meters of his own position. Considering that he had absolutely no training as a forward observer, Fujii became quite good at this dangerous profession before dawn came.

On the 20th, an all out rescue effort began with concentrated artillery fire and tactical air strikes on any possible enemy position near the fire support base. A fleet of 21 helicopters, under the command of Lieutenant Colonel William Peachey, orbited outside the battle area until the artillery barrage was over. The American forces were sparing no effort to get Fujii out of Laos. However, Fujii asked that the South Vietnamese wounded be evacuated first. Peachey turned down his request and ordered Fujii to get on the first ship that made it into the base camp. The US Army did not like the prospect of Fujii becoming a prisoner of war in Laos where American troops were not allowed.

In spite of the artillery, the ground fire was still intense. Peachey decided to send in a single helicopter rather than risk several. Major James Lloyd and Captain David Nelson flew out of the formation, hugged the tree line up the slope and dropped into the fire base. Fujii jumped on board, along with 14 wounded South Vietnamese.

The North Vietnamese did not have a chance to fire on the DUST OFF when it went in, but they made up for this oversight during its departure. Before the ship could depart, it took several hits. Seriously damaged, the helicopter made it out of the immediate combat area and crash-landed at a more secure South Vietnamese base camp four kilometers to the southwest. Everyone managed to get out of the burning ship before it exploded, miraculously avoiding injury. However, Fujii's new position came under attack shortly after he arrived. It took two days of steady fighting to finally get a DUST OFF in and fly him to the 85th Evacuation Hospital at Phu Bai. Aside from the Purple Heart for his wounds, the Army awarded Fujii the Distinguished Service Cross for his heroic performance on the ground inside Laos. Now, Dennis Fujii had joined the DUST OFF legacy.

DUST OFF had paid a heavy price for supporting Lam Son 719, which was the last major operation of the war supported by Americans. Six crewmen were killed, 14 wounded and 10 aircraft destroyed.

Although the Cambodian and Laotian operations were major offensive operations that inflicted severe losses on the enemy, the withdrawal of American forces continued as planned. To a large degree, Nixon had actually made Vietnamization work. In every aspect of the war, South Vietnamese soldiers were being trained and equipped to replace the Americans.

This was true with DUST OFF operations as well. By the summer of 1971, the Vietnamese Air Force was routinely flying DUST OFF missions in support of South Vietnamese Army units. In addition, Vietnamese pilots were being integrated into US DUST OFF units in order to get first hand experience on how the job should be done. Just like the Americans, the Vietnamese painted the big red crosses on their DUST OFFs. And, just like the Americans, they were getting shot up and shot down.

By now, it was painfully obvious that the distinctive red crosses on DUST OFF helicopters offered no protection from enemy gunners. Although several defensive measures had been taken to protect DUST OFFs, such as adding door gunners and requesting gunship escorts when possible, none of these steps reduced the rate of air ambulance losses; they only prevented the losses from reaching a prohibitive level. Still, the loss rate of DUST OFFs compared to all other helicopters was extremely high.

This growing concern finally led the Army to take a bizarre step in August, 1971, in a misguided effort to protect the DUST OFFs. Believing that making the aircraft even more distinctive might make them less vulnerable, the Army Medical Command in Vietnam was given permission to paint some of its aircraft white. Despite overwhelming evidence that the Viet Cong and North Vietnamese considered air ambulances just another target, there were those in the Medical Command that sincerely believed the enemy could be persuaded to change his tactics. While this scheme was hotly opposed within the DUST OFF units, the Army proceeded with its plan to make "albinos" of the DUST OFF fleet.

Thousands of posters were distributed and millions of leaflets dropped over enemy-held territory. While there were variations of the leaflets, the theme was always the same—please don't shoot at the white helicopters. The most elaborate leaflet read:

"Some new medical helicopters not only have Red Cross markings on all sides but also are painted white instead of green. This is to help you recognize them better than before in order to give the wounded a better chance to get fast medical help. Like all other medical helicopters, these new white helicopters are not armed, do not carry ammunition, and their only mission is to save endangered lives without distinction as to civilians or soldiers, friend or foe. Medical helicopters are used for rescue missions and they are not engaged in combat. You should not fire at them."

The Medical Command convinced the Psychological Operations folks that this idea had merit. From there, the idea of making mass leaflet drops really took off. By the 26th of September, the US Air Force 9th Special Operations Squadron had dropped over 5,000,000 leaflets. During the first week of October, 2,000,000 more leaflets fluttered to the ground. Unfortunately, the program did little more than blanket the country side with tons of paper.

On October 13th, DUST OFF 84 received an urgent request from a Popular Forces unit south of Tam Ky in I Corps. DUST OFF 84 was one of the integrated ships. The pilot was Warrant Officer Dave Martin and the co-pilot was Lieutenant Nguyen Van Hong. The crew of DUST OFF 84 piled in their shiny white albino and headed for the pick-up zone. It was supposed to be secure so they took no gunships with them. All went well until the aircraft was 30 feet from the ground. Then, all hell broke loose. DUST OFF 84 took fire from 360 degrees. Big, black ugly holes suddenly appeared in the white skin of the helicopter. Hong took rounds in his arm and leg; another one creased his neck. Martin immediately pulled in power and broke left away from the area, still taking intense fire until he was well out of range. As Martin raced to Tam Ky, which was six miles away, Specialist Vaughn, the medic, pulled the pins on Hong's seat and rocked it back so he could treat the co-pilot in flight. Vaughn managed to save Hong's life but the DUST OFF took over a dozen rounds in the process.

Clearly, the enemy would have shot at anything regardless of its color. In April, 1972, the North Vietnamese introduced the Russian SA-7 heat seeking missile into the war and promptly turned this 33-pound antiaircraft device against the white DUST OFFs. Between July 1st, 1972 and January 8th, 1973, the enemy knocked down seven albino DUST OFFs.

As it turned out, there was never any proof that painting the DUST OFFs white would provide any degree of protection. The idea was born of idealism, not reality. By 1972, it was patently obvious that the enemy, while well aware of the prohibitions against shooting down medical helicopters, shot them down as a matter of course. To believe he shot them down in error was extremely naive. Throughout the war, captured enemy soldiers told American interrogators that DUST OFFs were just another target. All said the only exception to the general policy of firing on all helicopters, regardless of mission, was to not shoot near base camps where the gunfire might attract too much attention to the area. One captured enemy soldier stated that the attitude in his unit was that red cross helicopters carried soldiers and it made no difference at all if they were wounded.

In any event, the SA-7 pretty much rendered the issue moot. In order to survive, the DUST OFFs were forced to fly at altitudes of 6,000 feet enroute to the landing zone and the hospitals. At this altitude, the enemy couldn't determine the color of the helicopters anyway. The only protection against the SA-7 was a new paint that reflected some of the engines heat away from the helicopter. When the paint dried, it was a dull charcoal gray.

In January, 1973, MACV directed that all DUST OFFs be painted with the new protective paint, which pleased most of the pilots. It wasn't exactly green, but it was far better that white. Thus ended the great experiment with white helicopters. They had not provided the protection the Army had hoped they would. In all fairness, they probably didn't do a great deal of harm, either. No cheap, easy gimmick could change the reality of the danger faced every day by the DUST OFF pilots. There was no "magic shield" or "silver bullet" for these guys. All the information available led to one inescapable fact—it didn't make a damn bit of difference what color the DUST OFFs were, they were going to be shot up and shot down.

By now, America's role in the Vietnam War was rapidly drawing to a close. As US combat units departed the war zone, so did the medical units. Vietnamization was moving forward at a rapid rate. By late 1972, most US combat units had departed or were ready to depart. The war was now in the hands of the South Vietnamese. It was going to be their war to lose; the Americans were going home.

Ironically, the last DUST OFF detachment to leave was the 57th. This was only fitting, since the 57th had been the first to arrive eleven years earlier. On the 11th of March, 1973, the 57th flew the last US DUST OFF mission in Vietnam—an appendicitis case. After turning in their helicopters on the 14th, the men of the 57th had nothing to do except wait. Some worked on their tan; others pretended they were already in the states and set their clocks accordingly. On the day they left Vietnam—29 March—MACV lowered its flag and ceased to function for the first time since 1962. America's war in South Vietnam was finally over. DUST OFFs were still flown by the South Vietnamese right up until the North Vietnamese invasion in April of 1975.

The Michelin Rubber Plantation, approximately thirty miles northwest of Saigon, was the scene of some of the fiercest fighting of the war. Here, the gound unit had to clear a landing zone by cutting down rubber trees.

10

The Value of DUST OFF

T he issues that caused America to go to war in Vietnam will be debated for genera
tions. However, there can be no argument concerning the significance of the DUST
OFF units. While the number of Americans killed in Vietnam exceeded 57,000, it is
entirely possible that this number could have been doubled had there been no DUST OFF.
As profoundly sobering as this statement is, it is absolutely true. This is why it is necessary
to look beyond what actually happened to truly appreciate the enormity of the contributions
made by the DUST OFF crews. In the end, this simple analysis is the finest tribute that can
be paid to the extraordinary men of DUST OFF, yet we have delayed for too long in paying
this tribute and making this analysis. However, it requires nothing more difficult than working the math. Numbers, at some point, matter. Evacuating nearly a million wounded, under
every conceivable condition, has to make a difference. And every mission flown was flown
the hard way. Every time a crew went up, somebody's ass was on the chopping block.

While mere statistics cannot come close to possibly describing the contributions made
by DUST OFF, they do allow us to put in perspective this incredible accomplishment.

From 1962 to 1973, a total of 496,573 DUST OFF missions were flown. Over 900,000
patients were airlifted from battlefields, rice paddies, destroyed villages, and triple-canopy
jungles, at all hours of the night or day, under all weather conditions, in the face of intense
enemy fire. While the primary objective of DUST OFF was the evacuation of wounded
American soldiers, everyone in the combat zone benefited from this extraordinary service,
even the enemy. Over the course of the Vietnam War, thousands of wounded Viet Cong and
North Vietnamese soldiers were saved by DUST OFF. The average time-lapse between
wounding and hospitalization was less than one hour. As a result, less than one percent of all
Americans wounded, who were able to survive the first 24 hours, died. These are unbelievably good numbers, yet somewhere along the way they have been lost by a nation completely self absorbed by the losses of Vietnam.

The surgeons at the evacuation hospitals often performed medical miracles on seriously wounded soldiers, and a great deal of the credit for the low mortality rate must go to
them. However, before the wounded could be saved they had to get to the hospital as quickly
as possible. It was this sense of urgency that drove the DUST OFF crews, and often they

paid a high price for their dedication. Over this eleven year span, over 200 crewmen were killed and many more were wounded. No record lists all of the DUST OFF pilots, crew chiefs, and medics who were wounded, and few document the bravery of those who died. At the peak of the war, only 140 helicopters out of a total fleet of more than 5,000 flew DUST OFF missions. Yet, these 140 helicopters made a critical difference. Flying DUST OFFs was three times more dangerous than all other forms of helicopter missions in the combat zone. This figure is borne out by the high rate of DUST OFF losses to enemy fire. During the course of the war, over 200 DUST OFFs were shot down by the enemy.

There is no question that these were truly exceptional men, performing on an exceptional level throughout the war. Yet, for the most part, they were quite ordinary before becoming a part of DUST OFF. In many respects, this is to be expected. They simply rose to the level required of them, which has always been a distinctive characteristic of Americans in combat. With DUST OFF, however, it was much more than this. There were other intangibles that went into building the DUST OFF legacy, creating an environment that drove these men to a level of performance far above what could reasonably be expected. Part of this can be explained by the realization that they were part of an elite organization that included such icons as Chuck Kelly and that they had extremely high standards to maintain.

While many of their peers back in the states were dodging the draft, burning the flag, and protesting the war, the DUST OFF crews simply kept flying missions, aware that their efforts were being jeered by an uninformed and ungrateful public at home. In spite of all this, they kept doing what had to be done. Perhaps this is the ultimate expression of courage, honor and dedication which defined the men of DUST OFF. In the end, however, nothing can fully explain these truly magnificent men.

By any measurement, flying half a million missions is a staggering accomplishment. Yet, all of this was accomplished by DUST OFF crews whose average age was barely twenty years old. In many states today, men that young can't even buy a beer or qualify for a credit card, or buy a car without a co-signer. For most, flying DUST OFF missions was the first real job they had ever held. They came in all shapes and sizes, from every state in the union, and represented every ethnic, social and religious group in the country. The crews included draftees, enlistees, and West Point graduates. Men from the coal fields of West Virginia blended easily with men from the wheat fields of Kansas and the oil fields of Texas. They all had hopes and dreams and plans for the future, just like everyone else. Some had girlfriends waiting for them when they returned, and others had wives and families. And when they crawled in the DUST OFF to fly the mission, none of this mattered. The only thing that mattered was the mission. And, because they were able to set aside every other consideration, they flew a half a million of them.

This could not have happened without something incredible to fly. For this reason, no tribute to the men who flew DUST OFFs would be complete without acknowledging the contributions made by the helicopter itself. Without question, the Huey proved to be equal to everything demanded of it. In many ways, it was the fifth member of the crew, often performing beyond expectations. It was sorely abused in untold thousands of evacuations, as the pilots pushed it to perform to the absolute limit. Along with the crew, the Huey took brutal, intense punishment, yet kept flying. This was not an easy aircraft to shoot down. It could take a lot of abuse and keep flying. In countless incidents, Hueys made it back so shot up that they should have been nothing more than smoking holes on the jungle floor. They made it back with holes in the main rotor, holes in the transmission, holes in the engine compartment, holes in the windshield, holes in the floor, and holes in the crew. They made it back with barely enough metal to hold the tail rotor on, radio shot up, instruments shot out, fuel gone, spewing oil, smoking, sometimes even on fire. But, against all odds, and in defiance of the laws of physics and aerodynamics, they made it back. Often, there was no explanation that made sense. Many pilots still swear that each Huey had its own personality, and that they were as close to being human as any machine will ever come. While this is open to debate, what cannot be debated is the bargain the US military received from Bell Helicopter.

Bell produced a tough, reliable helicopter worthy of the brave men that flew it. And, in the process, Bell has to receive a lot of the credit for the tens of thousands of good men who survived the war. Sometimes, things actually go right, and we all get lucky. Selecting the Bell prototype way back in 1955, when the Army went shopping for a new utility helicopter, was one of those times. No higher compliment can ever be paid to a defense contractor. Quality lasts, and it counts for a lot in combat. For this reason alone, Hueys will still be in the defense inventory well into the 21st century. Before the Huey is finally retired, it will have posted a service record spanning fifty years. Nothing lasts that long in the demanding military environment unless it pulls its own weight, and then some.

Still, none of these statistics captures the real essence of DUST OFF's contribution. Today, every major city in America has a medical evacuation capability modeled after DUST OFF. Countless thousands have been saved who would have otherwise died waiting for more conventional evacuation. There are people alive today, all over the world, who owe their lives to the men of DUST OFF. Many have no idea of the hard work and dedication that went into making DUST OFF a reality.

In the end, the only kind of legacy worthy of DUST OFF is a living legacy—the gratitude shared by thousands alive today because Temperelli, Kelly, and all those who followed flew the missions, during firefights, at night, in the middle of monsoons.....

Those Who Perished
(The Price That Was Paid)

The extraordinary accomplishments of DUST OFF did not come free. They were paid for, in blood, by some of the bravest, most dedicated men America has ever sent in harm's way. There was a price to be paid for saving nearly a million lives. To create the kind of living legacy that is DUST OFF, some very good men died. They died in the tradition created by Chuck Kelly, realizing that there was no such thing as a "safe mission" in a combat zone where the enemy had absolutely no regard for the internationally recognized rules of war. Under these conditions, every mission carried enormous risk, yet every mission had to be flown.

These are the men who understood the risk involved, and died doing what they did best—saving lives:

Major Charles L. Kelly, 57th Medical Detachment, 1 July, 1964
Specialist 5th Class Wayne C. Simmons, 57th Medical Detachment, 1 April, 1965
Captain Charles F. Kane, Jr., 1st Cav Division, 12 October, 1965
Private 1st Class Orin Allred, 498th Medical Company, 11 November, 1965
Private 1st Class William Esposito, 498th Medical Company, 11 November, 1965
Private 1st Class Gilivado Martinez, 498th Medical Company, 11 November, 1965
Warrant Officer George W. Rice, 1st Cavalry Division, 18 December, 1965
Private 1st Class Rudolph Jackymack, 1st Cavalry Division, 4 May, 1966
Captain Donald C. Woodruff, 1st Cavalry Division, 20 July, 1966
1st Lieutenant Dennis B. Easley, 1st Cavalry Division, 20 July, 1966
Specialist 5th Class Charles S. Rideout, 1st Cavalry Division, 20 July, 1966
Specialist 4th Class Clifford S. Bratcher, 1st Cavalry Division, 20 July, 1966
Private 1st Class Douglas M. Kyser, 1st Cavalry Division, 20 July, 1966
Major Kent E. Gandy, 254th Medical Detachment, 13 August, 1966
Major Harry Phillips, 254th Medical Detachment, 13 August, 1966
Captain Joe R. Fulghum, Jr., 283d Medical Detachment, 2 February, 1967
1st Lieutenant Alan Zimmerman, 283d Medical Detachment, 2 February, 1967
Specialist 4th Class Thomas M. Martinez, 283d Medical Detachment, 2 February, 1967
Private 1st Class Phillip H. Johnson, 283d Medical Detachment, 2 February, 1967
Specialist 4th Class Michael P. Kelley, 82d Medical Detachment, 16 March, 1967
Warrant Officer Ed L. Bush, 57th Medical Detachment, 20 March, 1967
1st Lieutenant Jack R. Lichte, 57th Medical Detachment, 20 March, 1967
Specialist 4th Class Ronald R. Fillmore, 57th Medical Detachment, 20 March, 1967
Private 1st Class Clifford R. Herrin, 57th Medical Detachment, 20 March, 1967
Captain Robert N. Bradley, 498th Medical Company, 21 March, 1967
Specialist 5th Class Dennis Ferrell, 498th Medical Company, 21 March, 1967
Private 1st Class Joel Fowler, 498th Medical Company, 21 March, 1967
Specialist 4th Class Ronald G. Trogden, 1st Cavalry Division, 19 June, 1967

1st Lieutenant Howard S. Schnabolk, 498th Medical Company, 3 August, 1967
Specialist 5th Class Dwight D. Woolf, 498th Medical Company, 4 August, 1967
Warrant Officer Roger C. Rose, 1st Cavalry Division, 8 September, 1967
Captain Kurt L. Kuhns, 1st Cavalry Division, 8 September, 1967
Specialist 4th Class Francis E. Gladibrook, 1st Cavalry Division, 8 September, 1967
Specialist 4th Class Dalton T. Goff, 1st Cavalry Division, 8 September, 1967
Specialist 4th Class Larry G. Lance, 1st Cavalry Division, 8 September, 1967
Specialist 4th Class Ramiro Herrera, Jr., 45th Medical Company, 22 September, 1967
Staff Sergeant Leroy Williams, 498th Medical Company, 25 September, 1967
1st Lieutenant Lawrence Gallego, 254th Medical Detachment, 4 October, 1967
1st Lieutenant David B. Wainwright, 254th Medical Detachment, 4 October, 1967
Specialist 5th Class Willie Green, 254th Medical Detachment, 4 October, 1967
Specialist 5th Class Roland H. Nielsen, 254th Medical Detachment, 4 October, 1967
Specialist 4th Class Ronald A. Martin, 254th Medical Detachment, 4 October, 1967
1st Lieutenant Robert G. Burlingham, 45th Medical Company, 6 October, 1967
Warrant Officer Robert G. Porea, 45th Medical Company, 6 October, 1967
Private 1st Class Joseph L. Hoggat, 45 Medical Company, 6 October, 1967
Private 1st Class Lewis A. Trask, 45th Medical Company, 6 October, 1967
1st Lieutenant Thomas J. Chiminello, 57th Medical Detachment, 29 October, 1967
Warrant Officer Forrest D. Raines, Jr. , 57th Medical Detachment, 29 October, 1967
Specialist 5th Class Lawrence Lano, 57th Medical Detachment, 29 October, 1967
Specialist 5th Class Herbert C. Donaldson, 57th Medical Detachment, 29 October, 1967
Major Larry G. Powell, 45th Medical Company, 22 November, 1967
Private 1st Class Ray Delgado, 82d Medical Detachment, 30 December, 1967
Warrant Officer Thomas A. Adams, 498th Medical Company, 31 December, 1967
Warrant Officer William G. Cheney, 498th Medical Company, 31 December, 1967
Specialist 5th Class Mario C. Lopez, 498th Medical Company, 31 December, 1967
Private 1st Class William D. Holland, 498th Medical Company, 31 December, 1967
1st Lieutenant Jerry L. Roe, 50th Medical Detachment, 12 February, 1968
Warrant Officer Alan W. Gunn, 50th Medical Detachment, 12 February, 1968
Specialist 5th Class Harry W. Brown, 50th Medical Detachment, 12 February, 1968
Specialist 4th Class Wade L. Groth, 50th Medical Detachment, 12 February, 1968
Specialist 4th Class James E. Richardson, 498th Medical Company, 4 April, 1968
Warrant Officer John Supple, 159th Medical Detachment, 29 April, 1968
Warrant Officer Thomas Pursel, 1st Cavalry Division, 19 May, 1968
Major William J. Ballinger, 45th Medical Company, 27 May, 1968
1st Lieutenant Guy T. Ephland, 45th Medical Company, 27 May, 1968
Specialist 4th Class Kenneth R. Rucker, 45th Medical Company, 27 May, 1968
Specialist 4th Class Alan L. Matte, 45th Medical Company, 27 May, 1968
Specialist 4th Class A. J. Dick, 1st Cavalry Division, 24 July, 1968
Warrant Officer Reinis Fox, 283d Medical Detachment, 4 September, 1968

Warrant Officer James G. Ziemet, 283d Medical Detachment, 4 September, 1968
Specialist 5th Class Charles L. Lumm, 498th Medical Company, 13 September, 1968
Warrant Officer Christopher D. Lucci, 498th Medical Company, 18 September, 1968
Specialist 4th Class Ronald T. Granville, 498th Medical Company, 27 September, 1968
Captain Robert E. L. Cottman, 82d Medical Detachment, 1 October, 1968
Warrant Officer Dennis Groth, 82d Medical Detachment, 1 October, 1968
Specialist 5th Class Ronald Doolittle, 82d Medical Detachment, 1 October, 1968
Specialist 5th Class Steven J. Saluga, 82d Medical Detachment, 1 October, 1968
Specialist 4th Class Richard W. Sanders, 82d Medical Detachment, 1 Octgober, 1968
Specialist 4th Class Calvin E. McGilton, 54th Medical Detachment, 3 October, 1968
Warrant Officer Timothy Cole, Jr., 54th Medical Detachment, 18 October, 1968
Warrant Officer Gary W. Doolittle, 54th Medical Detachment, 18 October, 1968
Specialist 4th Class Robert W. Dieffenbach, 54th Medical Detachment, 18 October, 1968
Specialist 4th Class Victor R. Hernandez, 54th Medical Detachment, 18 October, 1968
Specialist 4th Class David A. Wencl, 82d Medical Detachment, 3 November, 1968
1st Lieutenant Stephen C. Beals, 1st Cavalry Division, 26 November, 1968
Warrant Officer James D. Doran, 1st Cavalry Division, 26 November, 1968
Specialist 5th Class Johnny G. Greggs, 1st Cavalry Division, 26 November, 1968
Specialist 4th Class John Alling, Jr., 1st Cavalry Division, 26 November, 1968
Private 1st Class Robert E. Jones, 1st Cavalry Division, 26 November, 1968
Specialist 4th Class Charles E. Gay, 498th Medical Company, 15 December, 1968
Specialist 4th Class Teddy R. Sinninger, 498th Medical Company, 15 December, 1968
Warrant Officer Sylvester Davis, 283d Medical Detachment, 23 January, 1969
Warrant Officer Arvid O. Silverberg, 283d Medical Detachment, 23 January, 1969
Specialist 4th Class William R. Henderson, 283d Medical Detachment, 23 January, 1969
Private 1st Class Robert R. Sloppye, 283d Medical Detachment, 23 January, 1969
Captain Otha L. Poole, 45th Medical Company, 5 February, 1969
Warrant Officer William Hix, 45th Medical Company, 5 February, 1969
Specialist 4th Class Gary Johnson, 45th Medical Company, 5 February, 1969
Specialist 4th Class James McNish, 45th Medical Company, 5 February, 1969
Specialist 4th Class Kirk A. Wooley, 1st Cavalry Division, 12 February, 1969
Specialist 4th Class Gary L. Dubach, 1st Cavalry Division, 14 February, 1969
Specialist 4th Class Stephen L. Schumacher, 1st Cavalry Division, 14 February, 1969
Specialist 4th Class Richard J. Rochacz, 498th Medical Company, 22 February, 1969
Warrant Officer Douglas Stover, 254th Medical Detachment, 26 March, 1969
Warrant Officer Guy Johnson, 254th Medical Detachment, 26 March, 1969
Specialist 5th Class Carlos W. Rucker, 254th Medical Detachment, 26 March, 1969
Specialist 4th Class Gregory L. Habets, 254th Medical Detachment, 26 March, 1969
1st Lieutenain't Jerry T. Lee, 101st Airborne Division, 13 May, 1969
Specialist 4th Class James A. Margro, 101st Airborne Division, 13 May, 1969
Specialist 4th Class James R. Walters, 101st Airborne Division, 13 May, 1969

Warrant Officer Robert E. Layman, 54th Medical Detachment, 22 May, 1969
Warrant Officer Frederick S. Walters, 54th Medical Detachment, 22 May, 1969
Specialist 5th Class David J. Ewing, 54th Medical Detachment, 22 May, 1969
Private 1st Class Jeffrey A. Richardson, 54th Medical Detachment, 22 May, 1969
Warrant Officer Jonathan Vars, 1st Cavalry Division, 17 July, 1969
Captain George L. Miner, 101st Airborne Division, 17 August, 1969
Warrant Officer Gerald L. Cain'ton, 101st Airborne Division, 17 August, 1969
Specialist 5th Class James W. Megehee, 1st Cavalry Division, 7 September, 1969
Specialist 4th Class Gary L. Bowdler, 1st Cavalry Division, 7 September, 1969
Warrant Officer Roy M. Stilwell, 57th Medical Detachment, 30 September, 1969
Warrant Officer Orvala Baldwin, 101st Airborne Division, 5 October, 1969
Warrant Officer Rocky D. Armstead, 101st Airborne Division, 5 October, 1969
Specialist 5th Class Steven E. Arnold, 101st Airborne Division, 5 October, 1969
Specialist 5th Class Hubert D. Sutton, 101st Airborne Division, 5 October, 1969
Warrant Officer Fermen B. Hodges, 1st Cavalry Division, 28 October, 1969
Specialist 4th Class John P. Thrasher, 254th Medical Detachment, 4 November, 1969
Warrant Officer Don L. Rock, 57th Medical Detachment, 19 November, 1969
Specialist 5th Class Michael J. Poll, 498th Medical Detachment, 23 November, 1969
Captain Jesse A. Wisdom, 101st Airborne Division, 6 February, 1970
Warrant Officer Gard D. Thatcher, 101st Airborne Division, 6 February, 1970
Specialist 4th Class Richard F. Waltun, 101st Airborne Division, 6 February, 1970
Private 1st Class Morris Williams, 101st Airborne Division, 6 February, 1970
1st Lieutenain't Douglas G. MacNeil, 159th Medical Detachment, 7 April, 1970
Specialist 5th Class Loran E. Sweat, 283d Medical Detachment, 23 April, 1970
Warrant Officer Rodney K. Arnold, 1st Cavalry Division, 25 April, 1970
Sergeain't 1st Class James H. Brooks, Jr., 1st Cavalry Division, 25 April, 1970
Specialist 5th Class James T. Conway, 1st Cavalry Division, 25 April, 1970
Captain John R. Hill, 237th Medical Detachment, 27 April, 1970
Specialist 4th Class Zettie J. C. Dulin, 237th Medical Detachment, 27 April, 1970
Private 1st Class Randall W. Love, 237th Medical Detachment, 27 April, 1970
Warrant Officer John R. Smith, 45th Medical Company, 30 April, 1970
Specialist 5th Class John Keltner, 45th Medical Company, 30 April, 1970
Warrant Officer Alfred J. Gaidis, 237th Medical Detachment, 10 May, 1970
1st Lieutenain't Phillip N. Schmitz, 237th Medical Detachment, 10 May, 1970
Specialist 5th Class Charles A. Covey, 237th Medical Detachment, 10 May, 1970
Specialist 4th Class John A. Largent, 237th Medical Detachment, 10 May, 1970
Specialist 5th Class Theodore W. High, 254th Medical Detachment, 10 May, 1970
Specialist 4th Class Gary Taylor, 1st Cavalry Division, 24 May, 1970
Warrant Officer Bruce E. Graham, 101st Airborne Division, 26 May, 1970
Warrant Officer Edward T. OBrien, 101st Airborne Division, 26 May, 1970
Sergeain't David K. Johnson, 101st Airborne Division, 26 May, 1970

Specialist 4th Class William E. Hawkins, 101st Airborne Division, 26 May, 1970
Specialist 4th Class Kenneth H. Lamborn, 498th Medical Company, 9 June, 1970
Specialist 4th Class Jackson L. Wolfe, 254th Medical Detachment, 27 June, 1970
Specialist 4th Class Brent Law, 101st Airborne Division, 21 July, 1970
Warrant Officer William A. Parker, 498th Medical Company, 26 July, 1970
Specialist 4th Class David W. Maclurg, 237th Medical Detachment, 27 September, 1970
Warrant Officer Robert O. Hill, 237th Medical Detachment, 27 September, 1970
Warrant Officer Michael L. Bradley, 237th Medical Detachment, 27 September, 1970
Specialist 5th Class Kenneth C. Nokes, 237th Medical Detachment , 27 September, 1970
Specialist 4th Class Jeffrey M. White, 237th Medical Detachment, 27 September, 1970
Warrant Officer John L. Nesovonavic, 101st Airborne Division, 2 October, 1970
Specialist 4th Class Robert Alverson, 101st Airborne Division, 2 October, 1970
Specialist 4th Class Ronald K. Allgood, 101st Airborne Division, 2 October, 1970
Warrant Officer Gary W. Englehardt, 254th Medical Detachment, 17 October, 1970
Warrant Officer John R. Bregler, 254th Medical Detachment, 17 October, 1970
Specialist 4th Class Guy L. Mears, 254th Medical Detachment, 17 October, 1970
Warrant Officer Terrance A. Handley, 68th Medical Detachment, 20 October, 1970
1st Lieutenain't Kenneth M. Schlie, 54th Medical Detachment, 20 October, 1970
Specialist 4th Class Harold C. Gay, 54th Medical Detachment, 20 October, 1970
Specialist 4th Class Thomas R. Weiss, 571st Medical Detachment, 20 October, 1970
Warrant Officer Donald R. Cook, 498th Medical Company, 26 October, 1970
Warrant Officer Charles F. Smith, 498th Medical Company, 26 October, 1970
Specialist 4th Class Dennis E. Reese, 498th Medical Company, 26 October, 1970
Private 1st Class Karl L. Reineccius, 498th Medical Company, 26 October, 1970
Specialist 5th Class Gregory L. White, 54th Medical Detachment, 11 Novmber, 1970
Warrant Officer Paul R. Brass, 101st Airborne Division, 14 December, 1970
Warrant Officer Randall G. Freeman, 101st Airborne Division, 14 December, 1970
Specialist 5th Class Steve F. Johnson, 101st Airborne Division, 14 December, 1970
Specialist 4th Class Jeffrey D. Kuersten, 101st Airborne Division, 14 December, 1970
Specialist 4th Class John W. Murphy, 101st Airborne Division, 14 December, 1970
Warrant Officer Jospeh G. Brown, 237th Medical Detachment, 18 February, 1971
Warrant Officer John V. Rauen, 498th Medical Company, 20 February, 1971
Warrant Officer John Souther, 498th Medical Company, 20 February, 1971
Specialist 4th Class Dennis E. Gilliand, 498th Medical Company, 20 February, 1971
Specialist 4th Class John L. Levulis, 498th Medical Company, 20 February, 1971
Specialist 5th Class Russell G. Ahrens, 571st Medical Detachment, 18 March, 1971
Warrant Officer Hugh M. Pettit, 68th Medical Detachment, 10 April, 1971
Captain Thomas D. Chenault, 101st Airborne Division, 24 April, 1971
Sergeain't Jose A. Soto-Figueroa, 101st Airborne Division, 24 April, 1971
Specialist 5th Class Robert F. Speer, 101st Airborne Division, 24 April, 1971
Specialist 4th Class Johnnie R. Sly, 101st Airborne Division, 24 April, 1971

Warrant Officer Billy D. Pedings, 237th Medical Detachment, 15 June, 1971
Specialist 5th Class Donald Wood, 237th Medical Detachment, 15 June, 1971
Warrant Officer Chester A. Luc, 101st Airborne Division, 10 October, 1971
Warrant Officer Thomas J. Stanush, 101st Airborne Division, 10 October, 1971
Specialist 4th Class David J. Funes, 101st Airborne Division, 10 October, 1971
Specialist 5th Class Joseph M. Feeney, 101st Airborne Division, 10 October, 1971
Warrant Officer Ronald K. Schulz, 57th Medical Detachment, 13 October, 1971
Warrant Officer John S. Chrin, 57th Medical Detachment, 13 October, 1971
Specialist 4th Class Michael L. Darrah, 57th Medical Detachment, 13 October, 1971
Specialist 4th Class Hugo A. Gaytan, 57th Medical Detachment, 13 October, 1971
Private 1st Class Richard A. Pate, 57th Medical Detachment, 13 October, 1971
Warrant Officer Ain'thony J. Mensen, 54th Medical Detachment, 22 October, 1971
1st Lieutenain't William R. Lewis, Jr., 54th Medical Detachment, 22 October, 1971
Specialist 4th Class Billy V. Morris, 68th Medical Detachment, 22 October, 1971
Specialist 4th Class Ain'ton Schnobrick, 68th Medical Detachment, 22 October, 1971
Warrant Officer Robert L. Horst, 159th Medical Detachment, 7 April, 1972

Images

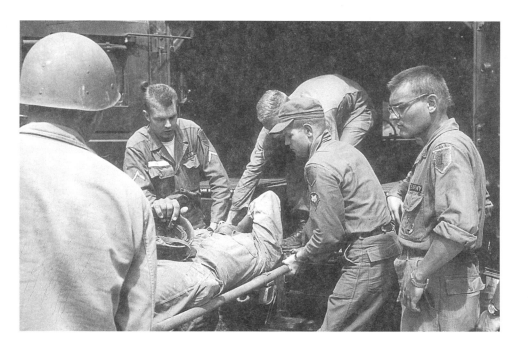

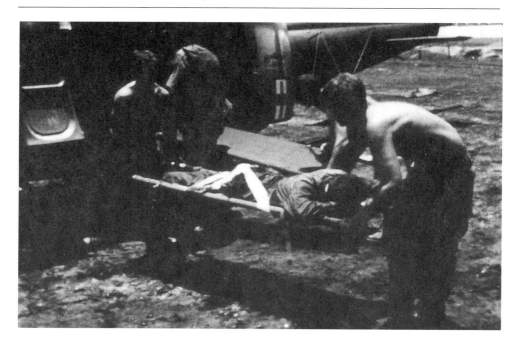

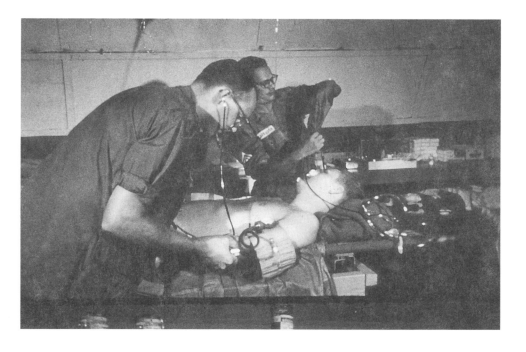

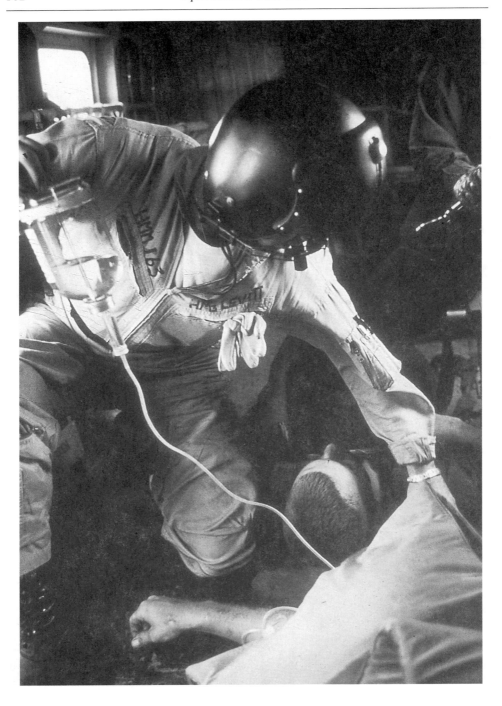

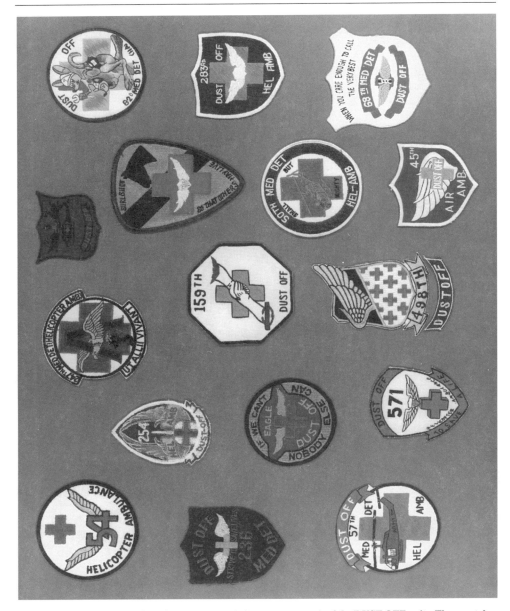

The Legacy of Kelly—Unit identity was extremely important to each of the DUST OFF units. These patches represent all the DUST OFF units assigned to Vietnam. They were worn with pride by all members of the crew. It is important to note that none of these patches were ever officially recognized by the US Army, yet no action was taken to discourage wearing them.

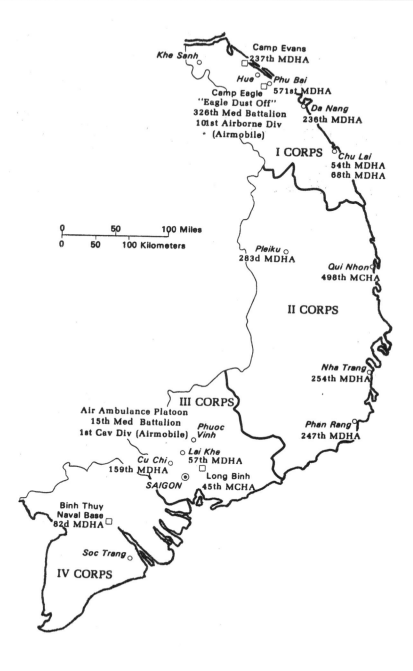

Camp Evans
237th MDHA

Khe Sanh

Hue
Phu Bai
571st MDHA

Camp Eagle
"Eagle Dust Off"
326th Med Battalion
101st Airborne Div
(Airmobile)

Da Nang
236th MDHA

I CORPS

Chu Lai
54th MDHA
68th MDHA

0   50   100 Miles
0   50   100 Kilometers

Pleiku
283d MDHA

Qui Nhon
498th MCHA

II CORPS

Nha Trang
254th MDHA

III CORPS

Air Ambulance Platoon
15th Med Battalion
1st Cav Div (Airmobile)

Phuoc
Vinh

Phan Rang
247th MDHA

Lai Khe
57th MDHA

Cu Chi
159th MDHA

Long Binh
45th MCHA

SAIGON

Binh Thuy
Naval Base
82d MDHA

Soc Trang

IV CORPS

This map shows the location of DUST OFF units in South Vietnam (See Unit Patches p. 168)

Index

H

Hanoi 48, 136
Haswell, Captain Edward 84
Hau Duc 112
Hiep Duc Valley 114
Horvath 133
Hueys 8
Hula, First Lieutenant Roger 84
Humphery, Hubert 126
Huntsman, Major 76
Huntsman, Major Howard 71

I

Ia Drang Valley 81
Iron Triangle 103

J

Jim, Lieutenant Troscott 77
Johnson 69, 73, 103, 118, 127, 128, 135, 136
Johnson, Lyndon 100, 118, 126
Jungle Penetrator 95
Jungle Platform System 94

K

Kane, Captain Charles F. 81
Kelly 5, 51, 52, 53, 54, 55, 56, 57, 58, 59, 60, 61, 62, 63, 64, 66, 67, 68, 69,
    70, 71, 74, 75, 76, 90, 93, 110, 111, 112, 115, 117, 125, 135, 148, 149, 150
Kelly, Major Charles L. 51
Kennedy 47
Kimsey, Captain Guy 81

L

Laos 140
Lloyd, Major James 143
Lloyd, Major Spencer 39
Lombard 100

THE ADVISOR-The Phoenix Program in Vietnam

Lt.Col. John L. Cook (USA, Ret.)

From his arrival in war-torn Vietnam in 1968 to his reluctant departure twenty-five months later, John Cook served as an advisor in the district of Di An and took part in the systematic operations of the Phoenix Program to destroy the the political organization of the Viet Cong and North Vietnamese forces. *The Advisor* tells how one man came to see the Vietnam War as *his* war, and how he learned the true costs of that freedom.

Size: 6" x 9", 70 color and b/w photographs, 3 maps

352 pages, hard cover

ISBN: 0-7643-0137-3

$35.00